Economic Growth, Development, and Foreign Trade

A STUDY IN PURE THEORY

Pranab K. Bardhan

Wiley-Interscience

A DIVISION OF JOHN WILEY & SONS, INC.

New York • London • Sydney • Toronto

Library of Congress Catalogue Card Number: 72-121903

ISBN 0 471 04830 5

Printed in the United States of America.

10 9 8 7 6 5 4 3 2 1

PREFACE

The market is full of books on trade and development. A customary function of the preface in still another book on a similar subject is, therefore, an attempt at product differentiation. It is not incorrect (or immodest) to assume, however, that such an attempt would be somewhat redundant in the present case. Even a casual look at the subsequent pages in this book will convince the reader of the narrowness of its purpose. The aim is to give a simple formal shape to some of the ideas often loosely discussed in the literature on trade and development. The focus is on analytic development on selected issues, not on new empirical insights or on comprehensiveness of treatment. In a field in which vague generalities abound, this may not be an entirely fruitless exercise. In fact I was strongly advised by a well-wishing friend to drop the disclaimer implicit in the subtitle "A Study in Pure Theory" in order to "rope in" some of the careless or habitual buyers of books on trade and development. On careful thought I chose to retain the subtitle, not because my marginal utility of money is low but because I dread the fury of deceived customers.

All this, however, should not convey the impression that the analysis contained in this book is overly rigorous. Far from it. In fact the mathematical purists may even find it rather loose. This is partly a matter of my competence, but also partly due to my aspiration to reach a somewhat larger audience. At this point I can almost hear my prospective reviewer pronouncing the ultimate judgment: "the author has resoundingly fallen between two stools."

This volume originated as a longish essay that was awarded the Stevenson Prize by Cambridge University in 1964, and I subsequently developed it into a doctoral thesis for the same university. In the process, I received very helpful guidance and criticism from my supervisors, James Meade and Frank Hahn. Then in 1966–68 I tried out some of the ideas outlined here on my students in graduate courses on trade theory at the Massachusetts Institute of Technology. It was a stimulating experience, and one of my students, Sydney Lewis, even became the co-author of Chapter 4 in the revised version. I would also like to acknowledge the assistance of two other M.I.T. students, David Scheffman and Vernon Renshaw, in revising the manuscript. In addition, discussions with and comments from Sanjit Bose, Murray Kemp, James Mirrlees, Robert Solow, and T. N. Srinivasan have been of great benefit to me in the preparation of various parts of this volume. But, needless to add, I am aware of the necessary loneliness of the error-maker.

PRANAB K. BARDHAN

February 1970
New Delhi, India

CONTENTS

INTRODUCTION

I.1. ON "DYNAMIZING" TRADE THEORY

From Smith to Keynes, most of the great economists of the past were actively interested in international trade, and many of their major contributions were directly connected with questions related to this aspect of economics. In contrast with this is the fact that most of the major advances in economic theory in recent decades have been based on the assumption of a closed economy. The pure theory of international trade, as developed in recent years, is, in spite of outstanding contributions here and there, not very strikingly rich in content and is rather narrow in its range (one reason, perhaps, why it is so frequently "surveyed"). Even when advanced techniques and methods have been developed in other branches of economic theory, trade theorists have often been slow to adopt and apply them in exploring new grounds. Some such feeling was the origin of the present study, but as will be obvious to even the most casual reader of the subsequent chapters we have not been able to proceed very far.

This book concentrates on certain problems of a growing open economy: in Part One we investigate the interelationships between various types of growth and foreign trade through descriptive models, and in Part Two we construct simple optimizing models that analyze trade, investment, and foreign exchange allocation policy in an intertemporal framework. The notorious historical lag with which trade theory has developed, as compared to the rest of general economic theory, has been particularly operative in this area. Although the interelationship between economic growth and international trade is one of the oldest themes in economics, until very recently there have been very few well-developed dynamic (as opposed to comparative-static) models in the literature. To quote from Haberler's survey [42], p. 58:

"As far as abstract theory is concerned there exists, however, not much more than occasional hints and programmatic pronouncements concerning the necessity of dynamizing traditional theory plus a few fumbling steps in the direction of the actual construction of dynamic models. Those who believe that it is possible to set up model sequences of economic development should go ahead and do it, instead of merely criticizing others for not having done it."

To quote from another survey by Caves [25], p. 242:

"Constructing models of international trade which involve time in some essential way (this is what we shall take 'dynamics' to mean) has become an activity uniformly approved but seldom practiced with success."

We have taken these statements of admonition and advice somewhat seriously.

In the last two decades, some important work has been done on dynamic models of trade; however, some of it consists of essentially isolated contributions[1] not well-suited to integration with the main

[1] One excellent example is the paper by Bensusan-Butt [17]. Since 1954 almost every writer on theoretical models of growth and trade has acknowledged it and duly recognized its important place in dynamic trade theory, but none, to our knowledge, has tried to develop the work any further or even tried a fuller exposition. Bensusan-Butt's model sequence of trade and accumulation is highly suggestive, but it would have been more easily followed up if it had been on a more rigorous and less impressionistic level. For fuller work on this line one has to cast it in terms of a fully developed vintage-capital model of the type analyzed by Solow [89] and others.

body of the pure theory of trade. As Bhagwati [19] aptly comments in his survey:

"In contrast to the general richness and synthesized character of much of pure theory in its comparative statics, dynamic propositions in international trade are comparatively few and bear no trace of any uniform design, each having been developed in virtual isolation. Dynamic trade theory, where it exists, has grown up in an essentially *ad hoc* fashion and has witnessed none of the inter-action of analysis which usually accompanies the development of an area of knowledge and produces a common design, a unifying frame."

One of the main purposes of this study is to consider some aspects of the impact of economic growth on the pattern of trade in terms of a very simple but roughly "unifying" framework.

I.2. THE MANY LIMITATIONS OF OUR STUDY

In Chapter 1, we review a large part of the results in the literature on the impact of comparative-static economic growth (capital accumulation and technical progress) on terms of trade, comparative advantage, real income, ratio of imports to income, and so on. In the Appendix to this chapter we derive corollaries to the results presented in the chapter in an analysis of the pattern of factor prices under free trade with international differences in production functions. Chapter 2 analyzes the necessary and sufficient conditions of complete and incomplete specialization in a model of capital accumulation. In Chapter 3 we examine two countries trading in consumer and capital goods, and from an analysis of the stability properties of growth equilibrium in this model we try to derive the time path of terms of trade and other variables. Chapter 4 presents two dynamic models, one involving imports of intermediate products not produced at home and the other dealing with imports of machines that are different from those produced at home; the first highlights the importance of the limitation of external demand for exports to the growth rate, and the second focuses on allocation of savings among heterogenous capital goods. In Chapter 5 we describe a fully developed model of heterogenous capital goods that considers embodied technical progress and economic obsolescence of machines;

we carry out a comparative-dynamic analysis of the impact of inter-country differences in wages, and hence in the economic lives of machines, on comparative advantage.

In Part Two some of the important intertemporal choices facing a simple growing open economy are considered. The social objective is to maximize a discounted stream of utility from consumption over a finite or infinite planning horizon. In Chapter 6 we discuss the two-sector, open-economy version of the standard one-sector, closed-economy, Ramsey-type model and analyze the optimum time path of trade and accumulation, once for the case in which there is instantaneous balance of trade and again for the case in which trade is balanced only over a given planning horizon, deficits of certain years being covered by borrowing from abroad and repaid in terms of trade surpluses in other years. Chapter 7 describes a dynamic model of "learning by doing" in an open economy in which production experience enhances productivity, and the optimum time paths of different variables, including that of the rate of subsidy ("infant-industry" protection) to the "learning" industry are analyzed. In Chapter 8 we consider a three-sector model in which capital once installed in a sector cannot be taken out and reinvested in another sector, so that different policies of allocation of foreign exchange give rise to different time profiles of consumption; on the basis of our optimality criterion, we try to determine the best way of allocating foreign exchange. Chapter 9 analyzes the optimum investment and trade policy in a dual-economy model in which the industrial sector obtains labor at a constant real wage from the agricultural sector and buys food from agriculture to feed industrial labor in exchange for selling manufactured consumer goods and agricultural inputs to farmers. In general, we have taken a fair number of what seem to be interesting theoretical problems involving dynamic issues of trade and investment and have tried to analyze them in the framework of very simple two- or three-sector growth models familiar in the current literature on growth and capital theory.

Undoubtedly we have left out important areas of trade theory that should be analyzed with dynamic models. For example, three such topics are: (a) the problem of analyzing much of international trade in manufactured products in terms of process and product innovations, research and development expenditure, human capital formation, and so on; there is a growing literature on this subject to which

Posner, Vernon, Hufbauer, Kenen, Keesing, and others have made important contributions (a large part of this literature has been surveyed and extended by Johnson [52]); (b) the related problem of explaining capital movements,[2] particularly among advanced countries, and the dynamic role of international corporations; and (c) dynamic economies of scale,[3] which are sometimes regarded as important determinants of international differences in productivity, and the related question of analyzing the growth benefits of economic integration and export expansion. In the last few years we have learned a lot, particularly in terms of empirical information, concerning these three classes of questions. From a theoretical point of view, however, the literature to date on these questions is somewhat disappointing. More often than not, the level of analysis is rather superficial and journalistic, and it often appears that a set of fairly obvious points are being belabored without a systematic study in depth into the various important questions that lie behind them. To be fair, this reflects on the state of general economic theory because it is impossible to visualize an adequate treatment of all the three classes of topics mentioned above without a satisfactory theory of generation and diffusion of technical progress and a viable general-equilibrium model that includes market imperfections and economies of scale. These are among the weakest points in available economic theory in general, and it is not surprising to find that trade theory shares these deficiencies. In this volume we do not propose to consider these issues.[4]

Apart from these omissions, we might mention some of the other general limitations of this study. First, ours is an exercise entirely in what is known, following Marshall, as "pure" theory of inter-

[2] Whenever we have discussed borrowing in this book (as in Chapters 6 and 9) this is more in the form of aid to a developing country.

[3] The only such scale economy we have considered in this book is that provided by "learning by doing" in Chapter 7. In general we have confined ourselves to the comfortable world of constant returns to scale.

[4] We might mention here, however, a direction in which a Vernon-type "product cycle" phenomenon in connection with international trade and investment can be fruitfully analyzed: there is a considerable scope for utilizing the results of Griliches and others on hedonic price indices, of Lancaster on the activity analysis of consumption, and of Houthakker on dynamic demand functions as building blocks for a theory of product innovations and quality changes and also a vintage model of consumer goods.

national trade. "Pure" in this context does not necessarily mean unadulterated by any sense of reality, but that monetary complications are ignored and we concentrate on "real" phenomena. We shall, of course, take one commodity as a unit of account, but in our model it does not also serve as a medium of exchange or a store of value. We shall not enter into the controversial discussion concerning the validity of the dichotomy between "real" and "monetary" in the neoclassical system; we shall instead take the convenient course and follow the standard practice of international trade theory in assuming that some of the important questions of long-run international trade can be posed—and at least partially answered—without referring to national currencies.

As is well-known from the critical literature on Heckscher–Ohlin theory, the two-country, two-commodity, two-factor model used in much, although not all, of this volume is severely limited in its usefulness. The traditional use of this model is based on a belief that it suggests "theorems which may be seen to admit of extension to more concrete cases," as Edgeworth [34], p. 31, says. Today, however, we enjoy the comforts of two dimensions with a very bad conscience, for restrictiveness of the results rapidly increases with each extra dimension. For example, in this study we frequently use a unique relationship between commodity and factor prices and repeatedly distinguish between goods intensive in different factors. As we all know, this becomes very restrictive indeed when any number of goods and factors are introduced. The introduction of more than two countries poses slightly less difficult analytic problems. Our assumption that both goods are being traded ignores important demand and supply relationships between the traded sector and the nontraded sector (for example, services) which always form an important part of any actual economy and whose importance may increase considerably with economic growth. The assumption of the absence of any nontraded good is partly connected with the assumption of no transport costs (in case of nontradeable services, transport cost is infinite); "distance" is not considered a factor in our model, as in most of international trade theory, much to the exasperation of location theorists.

We assume the price mechanism to be flexible enough to ensure full employment (except in Chapters 8 and 9) and balance-of-payments equilibrium. The familar Keynesian difficulties are ignored in our long-run model. In our discussion of continuous growth, full-employment savings are always equal to investment; all markets are cleared and any mistakes are instantly corrected, so that there is no divergence between planned and realized magnitudes. Thus, when we consider stability in our growth model in Chapters 3 and 4, our purpose is only to see whether or not any *equilibrium path* (along which savings equal investment and payments are balanced) converges to the steady-state path. Our dynamics is thus confined to what Hahn and Matthews [43] call "equilibrium dynamics." We ignore all errors of foresight and problems of uncertainty. In most of the chapters, we take capital as "perfectly malleable," but we relax this assumption in some significant ways in Chapters 5, 8, and 9.

Expectations of future developments play a more important role in determining the choice of techniques and the amount of investment when we depart from this assumption of perfect malleability of capital in Chapter 5; when capital is nonmalleable, an act of investment commits a hostage to the future. Even there, however, we assume that expectations (concerning movements in the wage rate, and so on) are correct and that they do materialize.

This is an array of breathtakingly "heroic" assumptions. Yet any student of current international trade theory will recognize them as very familiar assumptions. Because of the simple foundations of our basic model and its well-established role in static theory, we have found it to be of at least some heuristic value to set it "in motion" and work out its results, modifying it as required rather than building another *ad hoc* model from the ground up. Besides, as in many other purely academic but useful contributions to growth literature, our purpose is very much illustrative and is *not* to provide a model that is directly useful for understanding reality or for pronouncing policy judgments. In this connection we would like to quote from a recent survey of the theory of economic growth [43]:

"Different contributors to the theory of growth have differed a good deal in their views about the aims of the exercise. This makes for difficulty in drawing conclusions about how far the aims have been realized. Some authors have tried to construct models which, though simplified as any model must be, do correspond to the most important features of reality (the 'stylised facts,' in Kaldor's terminology), and they have proceeded to draw inferences about the explanation of observed events and about policy. Others have been less ambitious and have viewed their models as illustrations of how an economy *would* move on certain assumptions, in the hope that understanding of the laws of motion of their imaginary world might cast light, even if only by analogy, on the laws of motion of the infinitely more complex world of reality."

Our analysis is explicitly of the second, less ambitious, but probably not entirely trivial or useless, type. We believe that some of the questions asked, and sometimes even answered, at least partially, are important questions for a growing open economy.

PART ONE

Descriptive Models

I

ECONOMIC GROWTH AND TRADE—A COMPARATIVE-STATIC ANALYSIS

1.1. THE BASIC MODEL AND PROPERTIES OF TRADE EQUILIBRIUM

Starting with the description of a basic model in momentary equilibrium, we have two countries, the "home" country and the "foreign" country, two homogeneous commodities, c and m, and two homogeneous factors of production, labor (L) and capital (K).

The two static production functions are

$$F_i = F_i(K_i, L_i), \qquad i = m, c, \tag{1}$$

where F_i is the output of the ith commodity, and K_i and L_i are the amounts of capital and labor, respectively, employed in the ith sector.

The constant returns to scale assumption enables us to rewrite (1) as

$$F_i = L_i f_i(k_i), \qquad i = m, c, \tag{2}$$

where k_i is the capital-labor ratio employed in each sector. Both factors are freely transferable between the sectors, and assuming full employment,

$$\left.\begin{aligned} L &= L_m + L_c; \qquad L_m, L_c \geq 0 \\ &\text{and} \\ K &= K_m + K_c; \qquad K_m, K_c \geq 0. \end{aligned}\right\} \tag{3}$$

The supply of these factors is perfectly inelastic with respect to changes in factor prices.

In each sector the wage rate W is equal to the marginal value product of labor and the rental rate R is equal to the marginal value product of capital, if that sector's production is a positive amount. We take good c as the *numéraire*, so that its price is equal to unity. P is the international price of m in terms of c (in the absence of trade barriers, P is the same for both countries). The following marginal conditions determine factor prices:

$$R \geq F_{cK} \qquad \text{and} \qquad W \geq F_{cL}, \tag{4}$$

with the inequalities disappearing when output of c is positive, and

$$R \geq F_{mK}P \qquad \text{and} \qquad W \geq F_{mL}P, \tag{5}$$

with the inequalities disappearing when output of m is positive, where F_{ij} is the marginal product of the jth factor ($j = K, L$) in the ith sector ($i = m, c$).

From (2), $F_{iK} = f_i'(k_i)$ and $F_{iL} = f_i(k_i) - f_i'(k_i)k_i$. Substituting in (4) and (5),[1]

$$R \geq f_c'(k_c) \qquad \text{and} \qquad W \geq f_c(k_c) - f_c'(k_c)k_c, \tag{6}$$

and

$$R \geq Pf_m'(k_m) \qquad \text{and} \qquad W \geq P[f_m(k_m) - f_m'(k_m)k_m]. \tag{7}$$

Our assumption of positive but diminishing marginal productivity of factors implies that

$$\begin{aligned} f_i'(k_i) > 0 \qquad &\text{and} \qquad f_i''(k_i) < 0, \\ i = m, c \qquad &\text{for all} \qquad k_i > 0. \end{aligned} \tag{8}$$

[1] In this study a prime denotes the first derivative of a single-variable function; a double prime denotes the second derivative.

From (6) and (7), the wage-rentals ratio

$$w = \frac{W}{R} = \frac{f_i(k_i)}{f_i'(k_i)} - k_i, \tag{9}$$

if the ith sector's production is positive; $i = m, c$.

Equation (9) gives a unique relationship between the wage-rentals ratio and the technique (that is, capital-labor ratio, k_i) used in each industry. From (9),

$$\frac{dk_i}{dw} = \frac{-(f_i')^2}{f_i''f_i} > 0. \tag{10}$$

Equation (10) is positive in view of (8). This means that as labor becomes relatively more expensive, more capital is substituted for labor in each industry. In Figure 1.1, a familiar diagram of static trade theory used by Samuelson [83], Harrod [45], and Johnson [49],

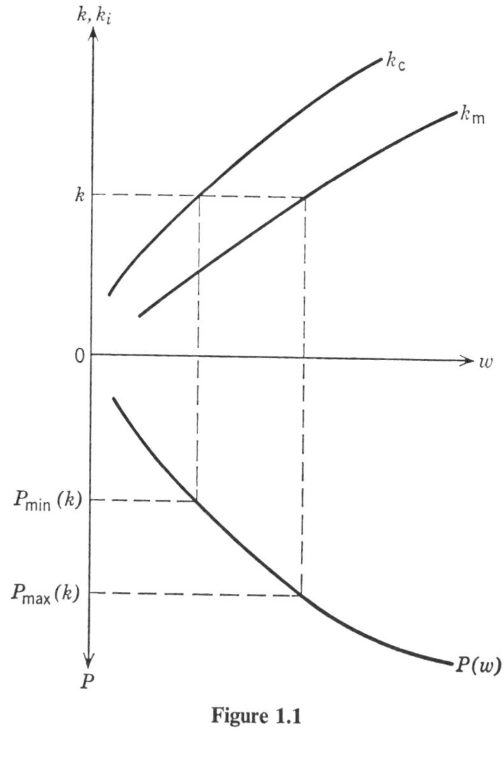

Figure 1.1

Chapter 1, the two curves in the upper quadrant express this relationship between sectoral capital-labor ratios and relative factor prices. The two curves, $k_c(w)$ and $k_m(w)$, do not cross as we assume nonreversal of factor intensities,[2] that is, a commodity that is, say, more labor-intensive in production is always so for all wage-rentals ratio.

If both sectors have positive output, from (6) and (7) we obtain the relative commodity price as the ratio of marginal products of each factor in the two industries, so that

$$P = \frac{f'_c[k_c(w)]}{f'_m[k_m(w)]}. \tag{11}$$

Logarithmically differentiating (11) with respect to w, using (9) and (10), and simplifying, gives

$$\frac{dP}{dw}\frac{1}{P} = \frac{(k_c - k_m)}{(w + k_m)(w + k_c)} \gtrless 0, \qquad \text{as } k_c \gtrless k_m. \tag{12}$$

With the assumption of nonreversal of factor intensities, (12) implies a unique relationship between commodity prices and factor prices when the country is incompletely specialized. This is one of the fundamental relationships in static trade theory, the essence of the Lerner–Samuelson factor-price equalization theorem.[3] The lower

[2] This assumption has been extensively discussed in the literature. Minhas [66] has tried to demonstrate, with the help of international cross-section data, that factor intensity reversals can be expected to occur within the empirically relevant range of wage-rental ratios often enough to vitiate the analytical usefulness of the conventional distinction between capital- and labor-intensive industries. Leontief's supplemental computation [60], pp. 339–343, on the basis of Minhas' own empirical evidence does not, however, seem to confirm the latter's conclusion. In fact it seems to confirm the conventional view. With two or three exceptions, each of the 21 industries considered may be characterized as being of uniform factor intensity. In a recent paper Ball [6] has noted that when agriculture and foodstuffs industries are removed from Minhas' tests, the rank correlation between factor intensities of Japanese and American industries increases considerably.

[3] It should be mentioned here that this unique relationship between commodity prices and factor prices is not in general valid for the many-goods, many-factors case without invoking restrictive assumptions. In the case of n commodities and n factors, a strongly *sufficient* condition—widely known as the Gale–Nikaidô [38] condition—for the global univalence of a differentiable mapping $\mathbf{p} = g(\mathbf{q})$, where $\mathbf{p}$ and $\mathbf{q}$ are n-dimensional vectors representing commodity and factor prices, respectively, is that the Jacobian matrix (with $\partial g_i/\partial q_j$ as its typical element) has all of its principal minors positive. For a good discussion of the problem, see Chipman [26] and Samuelson [84].

quadrant in Figure 1.1 shows this unique relationship between the wage-rentals ratio w and the commodity price ratio P, where it is assumed, for purposes of illustration, that c is the more capital-intensive good, that is, $k_c > k_m$.

From the full-employment condition (3), the capital-labor ratio of the economy as a whole k is a weighted average of the capital-labor ratios used in the two sectors, so that

$$k = \frac{K}{L} = k_m l_m + k_c(1 - l_m), \tag{13}$$

where $l_m = L_m/L$ is the proportion of the total labor force used in sector m.

Equation (13) implies that when the country is incompletely specialized (that is, both goods are being produced), the value of k is between those of k_m and k_c, whereas when $k = k_m$, $l_m = 1$ and the country is completely specialized in m; similarly, when $k = k_c$, $l_m = 0$ and $l_c = L_c/L = 1$, and the country is completely specialized in c.

In Figure 1.1, given k, the total capital-labor ratio of the home economy, its comparative cost range is the gap between what we have called $P_{\min}(k)$ and $P_{\max}(k)$. The pattern of specialization in the home country is determined by the relation between the world price P and these two critical prices:[4]

If $P \geq P_{\max}$, the country is completely specialized in producing good m, and $F_c = 0$.

If $P \leq P_{\min}$, the country is completely specialized in producing good c, and $F_m = 0$.

If $P_{\min} < P < P_{\max}$, the country is incompletely specialized, so that $F_c > 0$, $F_m > 0$.

The amount imported Z_i of the ith good is determined by domestic demand and supply conditions, so that

$$Z_i = D_i - F_i, \qquad i = c, m, \tag{14}$$

where D_i is the amount demanded of the ith good. The balance of trade (and payments as well, since for the time being we ignore foreign investment, and so on) is in equilibrium, so that

$$Z_c + PZ_m = 0. \tag{15}$$

[4] For a discussion of these limiting prices and the conditions of specialization in the Heckscher–Ohlin model, see Johnson [49], Chapter 1.

Equation (15) gives us the foreign trade transformation function[5] along which exports are "transformed" into imports through the world market.

All of the preceding discussion relates to the home country, but the same kind of relationships should hold for the foreign country as well. In subsequent discussions in this study, symbols relating specifically to the foreign country will be denoted by a bar above the corresponding symbols for the home country.

Let us now discuss the properties of stationary price equilibrium in the international market. Suppose dynamic behavior[6] "corresponding" to our basic static model is such that the rate of increase in P, the international price of m, varies monotonically with the world excess demand for m, E_m, and is zero when $E_m = 0$. We have the following differential equation for price movement in the world market:

$$\dot{P} = \theta[E_m(P)], \tag{16}$$

where an overdot denotes the time derivative, $\theta(0) = 0$, and $d\theta/dE_m > 0$. As a matter of fact, $E_m = Z_m + \bar{Z}_m$, where Z_m is the import demand for m by the home country and $\bar{Z}_m$ is the import demand for m by the foreign country (representing the rest of the world). In equilibrium,

$$E_m = Z_m + \bar{Z}_m = 0. \tag{17}$$

As can be seen from Figure 1.2, sufficient conditions for unique determination of a stable, positive, equilibrium world price P are indicated by

$$\frac{dE_m}{dP} = \frac{dZ_m}{dP} + \frac{d\bar{Z}_m}{dP} < 0 \tag{18a}$$

$$\lim_{P\to 0} E_m(P) > 0, \qquad \lim_{P\to\infty} E_m(P) < 0 \tag{18b}$$

Condition (18a) gives E_m as a continuously declining function of P

[5] The same function expressed as a relationship between imports of m (Z_m) and exports of c ($-Z_c$) gives the usual "offer curve."

[6] For other kinds of postulates concerning this dynamic behavior and for a more detailed stability analysis of the static trade model, see Kemp [54], Chapter 5, and Marshall [63], Chapter II.

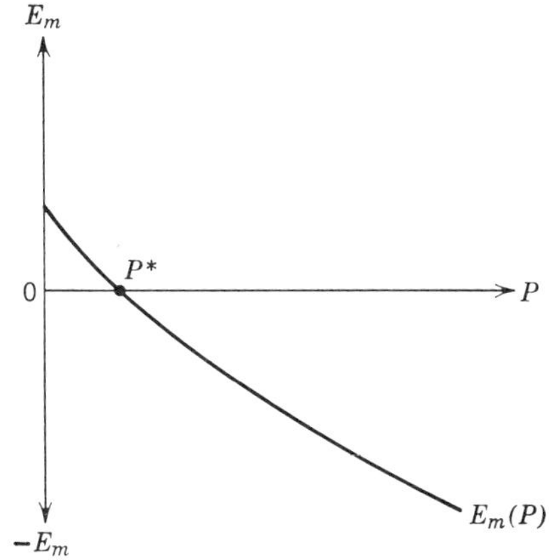

Figure 1.2

and thus ensures stability and uniqueness of price equilibrium P^*. For example, if we start with an initial P smaller than P^*, E_m is positive and hence from (16) $\dot{P}$ is positive, so P tends to converge to the unique P^*; likewise, for initial P larger than P^*. Condition (18a), by ensuring that the $E_m(P)$ curve starts from the upper quadrant and goes over to the lower quadrant, implies the existence of a finite positive P.

Condition (18a) actually corresponds to a familiar stability condition of trade theory. *Evaluated around equilibrium*, these conditions imply that the total price elasticities of demand for imports in the two countries add up to more than unity, which is the so-called Marshall–Lerner (local) stability condition.[7]

[7] This can be derived as follows. Suppose the home country is an importer of m, so that $Z_m > 0$. Take condition (18a), $dZ_m/dP + d\bar{Z}_m/dP < 0$, multiply by P/Z_m, use the equilibrium condition (17), and obtain the result that the total price elasticity (positively defined) of home demand for imports [that is, $-(dZ_m/dP)(P/Z_m)$] *plus* the total price elasticity of supply of exports of the foreign country [that is, $(d\bar{Z}_m/dP)(P/\bar{Z}_m)$] should be positive. Similar to (15), for the foreign country $\bar{Z}_c + P\bar{Z}_m = 0$, so that

$$\frac{d\bar{Z}_m}{dP}\frac{P}{\bar{Z}_m} = \left[\frac{d\bar{Z}_c}{d(1/P)}\frac{1}{P\bar{Z}_c} + 1\right].$$

This means that the total price elasticities (positively defined) of demand for imports in the two countries should add up to more than unity.

In most trade models this stability condition is taken for granted. Since price elasticity of industry output is usually non-negative (that is, $dF_m/dP \geq 0$) and "Giffen goods" are ignored (under the usual assumption of "gross substitutability" of the two goods c and m, $dD_m/dP < 0$), from (14), $dZ_m/dP < 0$, and if the same holds for the other country as well, (18a) is satisfied. Even when Giffen goods (in an individual budget) are absent, however, complications might arise if the distribution of income between the two factors of production affects demand. Recently Johnson [50] has analyzed a case in which substantial differences in the consumption propensities of the different groups of factor owners might vitiate the uniqueness and stability of international equilibrium. Let the price of importables rise; if now the owners of the factor that gains as a result (that is, the factor used more intensively in the importable commodity) have a very high marginal propensity to spend on the same (importable) commodity and the owners of the factor that loses have a very low marginal propensity to spend on it, then it might happen that a *rise in the price* of importables results in an *increased demand* for it. Thus, because of this redistribution-of-income effect, a good that is not a Giffen good to the individual might quite be one for the community as a whole. Under such "perverse" demand conditions in both countries, dE_m/dP might be positive and one might have instability and multiple momentary equilibria. This possibility, caused by perverse *demand* conditions, will, however, be precluded if supply conditions are sufficiently "normal," that is if the price elasticities of output are high enough. (As an exercise, the reader might confirm that if production functions are of the Cobb–Douglas type the equilibrium is unique and stable even if the income redistributive effect of price changes induce perverse demand response.)

In subsequent discussions we shall assume the stability condition to be satisfied.

1.2. COMPARATIVE-STATIC GROWTH AND TERMS OF TRADE

Given the stability of a unique momentary equilibrium in our model, we can now discuss various comparative-static questions regarding the impact of different patterns of economic growth.

Suppose we are interested in finding the impact of a particular type of growth on the terms of trade of the home economy. Take m to be the importable good and c the exportable good for the home economy.[8] The terms of trade are then given by the reciprocal of P. We know from (17) that in equilibrium $Z_m(\alpha, P) + \bar{Z}_m(P) = 0$, where α represents a shift parameter representing economic growth and the foreign country is assumed to be static (this assumption will be relaxed later). Then,

$$\frac{dP}{d\alpha} = \frac{\dfrac{\partial Z_m}{\partial \alpha}}{-\left[\dfrac{\partial Z_m}{\partial P} + \dfrac{d\bar{Z}_m}{dP}\right]}. \tag{19}$$

From (18a) we know that the stability condition implies that the denominator on the right-hand side of (19) is positive, so that $dP/d\alpha$ has the same sign as $\partial Z_m/\partial\alpha$. In other words, given stability of equilibrium and given a static foreign country, economic growth will change the world price P in the same direction as it changes the demand for imports of m for the home economy *at the initial terms of trade*. If economic growth increases the demand for imports of m at the initial prices, P will go up, which means a decline in the home country's terms of trade. Let us try to determine the cases in which economic growth increases the demand for imports of m. With incomplete specialization the demand for imports of m is equal to the amount domestically demanded *minus* the amount domestically produced. So if we start with positive initial imports of m, economic growth will increase the demand for imports of m at the initial terms of trade, if the rate of growth of domestic demand for m is not lower than that of domestic production of m at constant prices. We shall now try to find cases in which this happens.

Let us first take the case in which the only type of growth involved is that of a (once-and-for-all) increase in the capital stock per unit of labor (that is, k) for the home economy. How does this affect output at the same initial prices? Since commodity prices

[8] We shall, for the time being, assume that economic expansion is small enough not to reverse the comparative advantage pattern, so that m continues to be the home country's importable good.

are kept the same, factor prices will remain constant because of the unique relationship between factor prices and commodity prices in this model with incomplete specialization, as seen from (12); if factor prices are constant, the capital labor ratio used in each industry k_i will remain constant because of the unique relationship between factor prices and sectoral factor proportions, as seen from (10). This is a case in which the capital-labor ratio of the economy as a whole has increased, but the capital-labor ratios used in each industry remain the same. If full employment of both factors is to be maintained, the increase in the economy's total capital-labor ratio is to be absorbed only by a shift in weight (say, the proportion of the total labor force that is employed in each industry) in favor of the more capital-intensive industry. This means an increase in the relative output level of c, if we assume c to be the more capital-intensive good. If the labor supply is fixed, so that only capital has grown, this shift in weight means an absolute reduction in output of the more labor-intensive industry m. This is generally referred to as the Rybczynski [80] theorem. A similar reduction in output of m follows even if the labor supply is not fixed, but grows at a sufficiently lower rate than capital.

An equational derivation of these results is not difficult. From (13), when k_m and k_c are constant,

$$\dot{k} = -\dot{l}_m(k_c - k_m), \tag{20}$$

where an overdot indicates a time derivative. This means that if the capital-labor ratio k of the economy goes up but prices remain constant, and if c is the more capital-intensive good, then the proportion of the total labor force used in the more labor-intensive industry m, l_m, goes down.

From (2), the output of industry m is given by

$$F_m = Ll_m f_m(k_m). \tag{21}$$

From (20) and (21), the output of m goes down at the initial prices if capital grows with a fixed labor supply.

The output of good c relative to m is given by

$$\frac{F_c}{F_m} = \frac{(1 - l_m)f_c(k_c)}{l_m f_m(k_m)}. \tag{22}$$

From (20) and (22), the *relative* output of the capital-intensive good

c goes up (remains the same) if the capital-labor ratio of the economy goes up (remains the same) with prices constant.

From (13),

$$l_m = \frac{k_c - k}{k_c - k_m}. \tag{23}$$

It is easy to confirm from (20), (21), and (23) that the output of the labor-intensive good m will go down if

$$\frac{\dot{K}}{K} > \frac{\dot{L}}{L}\frac{k_c}{k}. \tag{24}$$

In other words, if labor also grows, but at a rate sufficiently lower than capital, then at constant prices output of the more labor-intensive good will go down. This is a slight generalization of the Rybczynski result,[9] which is for the case of $\dot{L}/L = 0$.

For all these cases in which output of the importable good m goes down, economic growth raises the demand for imports of m at the initial terms of trade unless m happens to be a strongly "inferior" good in the consumer budget. Except for the case of inferior goods, economic growth does not depress domestic demand for m at con-

[9] For a geometric derivation of this result, see Guha [41]. It might also be mentioned that the strong Rybczynski theorem does not hold for the general case of many goods and many factors. The problem, briefly stated, is as follows. The Rybczynski theorem implies that if there is an increase in the factor endowment of the ith factor, all other factor endowments remaining the same and prices remaining constant, there will be a more than proportionate increase in the output of the ith good that is in some sense "intensive" in the ith factor. With given commodity and factor prices, the (logarithm of the) amount of each factor employed will be a function of the (logarithm of the) quantities of all the goods produced. The Jacobian matrix of this function will have its (i, j) element representing the percentage change in quantity of factor i required to produce a percentage change in the output of industry j; this is equal to the fraction of the ith factor used in the jth industry. Thus, the Jacobian matrix is a stochastic matrix, since all the elements are non-negative and the row sums equal unity. If one takes the inverse of this matrix, the (i, j) element of that matrix will represent the total effect of a percentage change in ith factor endowment on the output of the jth commodity. The Rybczynski theorem in effect states that the principal-diagonal elements in this inverse matrix are greater than unity. For the inverse of a stochastic matrix to have this property requires some very stringent conditions which are not assumed in the Rybczynski model. In this sense the theorem is not generalizable. For a more detailed discussion, see Minabe [65].

stant prices, and if the latter's output falls, demand for imports goes up at the initial terms of trade. From (19), this means that the terms of trade decline for the home country.

What happens to demand for imports of *m* and thus to terms of trade in the case in which the output of *m* does not fall absolutely but only relatively to the output of *c* at constant prices? This is the general case that arises when capital grows at a higher rate than labor. Obviously the answer also depends on the income elasticity of demand. If the income elasticity of demand (defined at constant prices) for *m* is equal to (greater than) unity, then domestic demand for *m* at constant prices will grow at the same (higher) rate as the national income, whereas on the supply side domestic output of *m* at constant prices grows at a rate *lower* than that of the national income, because the rate of growth of national income and output is a weighted average of the rates of growth of the outputs of the two industries. In this case once again, economic growth raises the demand for imports at constant prices and thus turns the terms of trade against the country. The same result obviously follows in the case in which capital and labor grow at the same rate.

Let us now introduce growth in the form of technical progress[10] in this model and ignore accumulation of factors. We shall first determine its impact on domestic production at constant prices. Technical progress in an industry is defined as Hicks-neutral, capital-saving, or labor-saving as it leaves unchanged, decreases, or increases the capital-labor ratio employed at the initial wage-rentals ratio. Suppose, to start with, technical progress occurs only in the more capital-intensive industry *c* and that there is no technical change in industry *m*. This reduces the relative cost of production of *c* at the initial wage-rentals ratio, but if commodity prices are to be kept constant, the relative cost of producing *c* must be pushed up by a rise (for a diagrammatic representation see the Appendix to this chapter) in the relative cost of capital (the factor used more intensively in industry *c*). The resulting fall in the wage-rentals ratio tends to lead to the use of higher labor-capital ratios in *both* industries. Apart from this indirect effect of technical progress in industry *c* at constant commodity prices on capital-labor ratios employed in each industry through changes in the wage-rentals

[10] This means production functions in (1) are now changed to $F_i = F_i(K_i, L_i, t)$, where F_i is homogeneous of degree one in K_i and L_i, and $\partial F_i/\partial t > 0$.

ratio, there is the direct effect of the nature of technical progress on the capital-labor ratio of the changing industry at the same wage-rentals ratio. When technical progress in industry c is Hicks-neutral or capital-saving, if one takes account of both the direct and indirect effects, capital-labor ratios in *both* industries will go down compared to the initial situation. Under these circumstances the maintenance of full employment of the given endowment of factors can be reconciled with a fall in the capital-labor ratios in both industries only by a shift of resources to the capital-intensive industry and away from the labor-intensive industry[11] leading to, in this case, an absolute decline in the output of the labor-intensive good m at the initial prices. Thus, as in the Rybczynski case involving factor accumulation, in this case also economic growth raises the demand for imports of m at the initial terms of trade (since output of m falls while the demand increases at constant prices, unless m is an "inferior" good). From (19) this means that the terms of trade decline for the growing country.[12]

What happens if technical progress in capital-intensive industry c is labor-saving? In this case the direct effect of technical progress tends to raise capital-labor ratio employed in industry c for a given wage-rentals ratio, but the indirect effect of technical progress at constant prices is, through a fall in the wage-rentals ratio, to lower the capital-labor ratios employed in both industries. The net effect on the capital-labor ratio in industry c is ambiguous unless one introduces further assumptions about the relevant parameters (such as the extent of labor-saving bias of technical progress, the elasticity of substitution, and so on), as is the effect on output of m.[13]

In cases in which the output of the importable good m does not decline at constant prices, or more generally, when there is technical

[11] From (13), $\dot{k} = \dot{k}_m l_m + \dot{k}_c(1 - l_m) - \dot{l}_m(k_c - k_m)$. With $\dot{k} = 0$ since we have excluded accumulation of factors, with $\dot{k}_m < 0$, $\dot{k}_c < 0$ since capital-labor ratios decline in both industries, and with c the more capital-intensive industry, l_m the proportion of labor used in m industry, goes down and, hence, output of m falls.

[12] This result is attributable to Findlay and Grubert [37] and Johnson [51], Chapter 4.

[13] In terms of footnote 11, we are no longer sure of the sign of $\dot{k}_c$ and therefore of that of $\dot{l}_m$.

In Bardhan [12] it is shown how a simple restriction on the extent of labor-saving bias of technical progress in industry c is sufficient for an absolute reduction in the output of m.

progress in industry m as well, as in the case of general factor accumulation, we need more information about demand. If, for example, income elasticity of demand for m is greater than (equal to) unity, domestic demand for m at constant prices grows at a rate higher than (the same as) national income, and if on the supply side domestic output of m at constant prices grows at a rate lower than (or equal to) that of c and therefore of national income (since the growth rate of national income at constant prices is just the weighted average of the growth rates of the two industry outputs), economic growth would once again raise the demand for imports at constant prices and thus lead to a downward equilibrating movement in terms of trade of the growing country. With the help of footnote 10 and with the classification of technical progress in mind, the reader may easily confirm that this will happen if Hicks-neutral or capital-saving technical progress in both industries occurs at the same rate or at a higher rate in the more capital-intensive industry c.

We have so far assumed the foreign country to be static. The method of analysis, however, remains the same when there is simultaneous growth in both countries. Given the stability condition (18), (19) can now be restated as

$$\operatorname{sign}\frac{dP}{d\alpha} = \operatorname{sign}\left[\frac{\partial Z_m}{\partial \alpha} + \frac{\partial \bar{Z}_m}{\partial \alpha}\right]. \tag{25}$$

For an illustrative exercise let us take the case in which capital is growing at a rate no less than that of labor and there is no technical change. Noting (14) and (17), and that at constant prices the rate of growth of demand for m is given by income elasticity of demand for m multiplied by the rate of growth of national income we can write

$$\frac{\partial Z_m}{\partial \alpha} + \frac{\partial \bar{Z}_m}{\partial \alpha} = (e_m - 1)D_m \hat{Y} + (\hat{Y} - \hat{F}_m)F_m + (\bar{e}_m - 1)\bar{D}_m\hat{\bar{Y}}$$
$$+ \bar{F}_m(\hat{\bar{Y}} - \hat{\bar{F}}_m) + Z_m(\hat{Y} - \hat{\bar{Y}}), \tag{26}$$

where e_m is income elasticity of demand for m in the home country, Y is national income in the home country, overbars represent the foreign country, and a caret indicates the proportionate rate of growth of the variable underneath at constant commodity prices.

We have already noted that when capital grows at a rate higher than (equal to) that of labor, the output of the labor-intensive good m grows at a rate lower than (equal to) that of the other commodity, and hence that of national income. This implies that $\hat{Y} > \hat{F}_m$ and $\hat{\bar{Y}} > \hat{\bar{F}}_m$. Thus, the right-hand side of (26) is positive if (a) income elasticity of demand for m in either country is not less than unity and (b) the rate of growth of national income in the home country is not less than that abroad. Under these sufficient conditions, terms of trade will deteriorate for the home country importing m.

Other Effects of Growth. We have so far been concerned with the impact of growth on terms of trade. With the help of the discussion above one may try to answer more general questions, such as those involving the impact of growth on real national income or on the "import dependence" of the economy (as measured by the ratio of value of imports to national income). We shall very briefly consider these problems.

Let us take the second problem first. Several attempts have been made in the empirical trade literature to find out how economic growth has historically affected the ratio of foreign trade to national income.[14] In a simplified comparative-static form, this question can be theoretically analyzed in terms of our model. More formally, we have to determine how the ratio PZ_m/Y is affected by different types of economic growth. We shall illustrate this problem for the simplest case, leaving probably the more interesting cases as more elaborate, but not difficult, exercises for the reader. Suppose that in the home economy capital and labor are growing at the same rate and/or Hicks-neutral technical progress is occurring at the same rate in both industries (again assuming the foreign country to be static). Suppose also that the income elasticity of demand for importable good m is unity. From our discussion above we know that in this case output at constant prices grows at the same rate in both industries (as does national income at constant prices), and thus terms of trade decline or the world price of m, P, goes up. Since in this case growth at constant prices leads to a constant output ratio F_m/F_c, and since as P, the relative price of m, goes up the relative production of m should go up,[15] we can say that in this case growth leads to a rise in PF_m/F_c or a fall in PF_m/Y, the value of output of m as a proportion

[14] For a good summary of the literature, see Kindleberger [57], Chapter 11.

[15] It is easy to see this if one draws a transformation curve for F_m and F_c and slides along the price line tangent to it.

of national income. What happens to PD_m/Y, the proportion of national income spent on m? Since income elasticity of demand for m is assumed to be unity, growth keeps PD_m/Y constant if prices are constant, but since P goes up the net effect will be a *fall* in PD_m/Y if price elasticity of demand for m is, in absolute value, not smaller than unity. Thus, if PD_m/Y falls and PF_m/Y rises, from (14) it is clear that PZ_m/Y should fall, that is, the ratio of value of imports to national income goes *down* in this particular case.

As for the impact of growth on real national income, we shall be briefer. We have seen some cases of economic growth in the home country that will lead to an adverse movement in its terms of trade. This suggests the possibility, first noted by Edgeworth [33], that growth may turn out to be "damnifying" for a country. If the gain in real income on account of economic growth at the initial terms of trade is outweighed by the loss of real income (measured, as an approximation usual in international trade theory, by the excess cost of buying the initial amount of imports, that is, $\dot{P}Z_m$ for the m-importing country) on account of the consequential adverse shift in terms of trade, then, under free trade, the growing country will suffer a net loss of real income. This case has been considered at some length in the literature,[16] where sufficient conditions for such a possibility are spelled out. We may only mention here that in general these conditions are quite stringent, making it very unlikely.

1.3. GROWTH AND COMPARATIVE ADVANTAGE

Finally, let us say a few words on the impact of technical progress on comparative advantage. It is very easy to formulate generalized Ricardo–Heckscher–Ohlin models in which both factor endowments and technical knowledge affect productivity (see, for example, Amano [1], Bardhan [8]), and depending on the relative rates of technical progress in the two industries we can derive general propositions about the international distribution of comparative advantage. It is, however, more difficult to go beyond these models and construct a satisfactory theory concerning the generation of technical knowledge itself and its sectoral distribution pattern. In other words, it is desirable to investigate the factors that cause the so-called

[16] See, for example, Bhagwati [18].

"technological gaps" between advanced and relatively backward countries and also to find out why the gap is larger in some industries and smaller in others.

Let us briefly comment on three types of considerations which might be important in this context. One is the suggestion that capital-rich countries can afford to save and invest more in the formation of skills embodied in labor and in research and development activities. This is not enough, however, to explain why the benefits of improved technology or improved human skills help some industries more than others, and without such an explanation one cannot fully explain *comparative* advantage.

A second suggestion involves the phenomenon of learning by doing. Arrow [3] has introduced a growth model in which labor efficiency is an increasing function of the cumulated volume of gross investment (that is, the integral of all past investment). The production function of the ith good in this model is

$$F_i = F_i(K_i, A(K)L_i), \qquad i = c, m, \tag{27}$$

where A is the labor-efficiency-augmenting term[17] that depends on K, the country's total stock of capital (equal to the integral of all past investment, assuming, for simplification, the absence of depreciation). Following Arrow, we can assume a specific form of the $A(K)$ function:

$$A(K) = aK^n, \qquad 1 > n > 0; \tag{28}$$

n, the learning coefficient, being less than unity implies that there are diminishing returns to learning.

We can now substitute (27) and (28) in (1) and carry out the same sort of analysis outlined in Section 1.1 to obtain an equation for P, the relative price of m in terms of c, as a ratio of marginal products of capital in the two industries (by assuming that the learning effect comes as an external economy to an individual firm, we can retain all our competitive assumptions). Logarithmically differentiating this equation with respect to time, we obtain

$$\frac{\dot{P}}{P} = \frac{\dot{A}}{A}(Q_c - Q_m) + (Q_m - Q_c)\frac{\dot{w}}{w}, \tag{29}$$

[17] In Arrow's vintage-capital model the learning effect benefits only the new machines; here we are ignoring this additional complication of his model and concentrating on his basic idea of a learning function.

where Q_i is the wage-share in the ith industry and w is the wage-rentals ratio. If m is the labor-intensive good, $Q_m > Q_c$. The right-hand side of (29) has two terms, the first indicating the effect of learning on prices and the second indicating the usual Heckscher–Ohlin effect of factor prices on commodity prices. In the absence of the learning effect (that is, when $\dot{A} = 0$), the country with the higher wage-rentals ratio (usually the capital-abundant country) has a higher P (the relative price of the labor-intensive good m). If one ignores the Heckscher–Ohlin effect, however, and concentrates on the first term involving $\dot{A}$, an opposite result is obtained in this case. Since $\dot{A}/A = n(\dot{K}/K)$ and $Q_m > Q_c$, the country with the larger capital stock will tend to have a lower relative price for the labor-intensive good. The net effect on comparative advantage, of course, will be the outcome of these two conflicting influences on P. But let us only note here that with the learning function taken here the capital-abundant country will tend to have a relative *efficiency advantage* in the labor-intensive good.[18]

We can obtain a similar result if instead of the learning function (28) we introduce the concept of education speeding technological diffusion.[19] Let us suppose that the labor-efficiency-augmenting term $A(t)$ in the production function is given by

$$A(t) = ae^{\lambda[t-g(k)]}, \qquad g'(k) < 0, \tag{30}$$

where λ is the rate at which technology is advancing and g is the time lag between the theoretical availability of a new technique and its adoption. We have in mind a model in which the higher the level of education of a country's population, the shorter the lag with which it adopts new technology. We assume g to be a decreasing function of k, the capital-labor ratio of the country, to indicate that the country with the higher capital-labor ratio can afford to have more education and therefore a smaller time lag g.

Putting (30) in (29), we can once again say that in this model the country with the higher capital-labor ratio will tend to have a relative efficiency advantage in the more labor-intensive good.

An extension of the idea incorporated in (30) leads us to a third

[18] There is some empirical evidence for this in international productivity data; see Arrow et al. [4] and other references cited in footnote 24. See Kenen [55] for a distinct but related explanation of the same phenomenon.

[19] See Nelson and Phelps [71].

type of explanation of the technological gap and the pattern of comparative advantage. If we have a vintage-capital model in which technical progress is embodied only in new machines, then the speed with which new technology is adopted will depend on the rate at which old machines are scrapped, which in turn depends on wage rates. Thus, even if the same technology on new machines is available to all countries, because of different wages and hence different economic lives of machines different countries will have different relative productivity. This is the subject of our analysis in Chapter 5.

APPENDIX

International Differences in Production Functions, Trade and Factor Prices

In Sections 1.2 and 1.3 we discussed the impact of technical progress on terms of trade and on comparative advantage. However, we ignored one important by-product of that analysis, namely, its implications for the analysis of factor prices under free trade with international differences in production functions. In the standard Heckscher–Ohlin–Samuelson analysis of factor prices under free trade, production functions are assumed to be internationally identical. There is very little discussion in the literature[20] about the international pattern of factor prices in the case in which this grossly unrealistic assumption is relaxed. This appendix is devoted to the question.

We start by analyzing the implications of technical change *at constant commodity prices* for an isolated economy and find out how between two situations I and II with technical change, factor prices change in the second posttechnical-change situation with commodity prices remaining the same. Then instead of considering the two situations I and II as succeeding states of the same isolated economy, we consider them as representing two economies under free international trade at a point in time. In other words, the distinction in time is replaced by a distinction in space (assuming, as we have done throughout this book, that transport is costless). In the "intertemporal" case commodity prices are assumed to be constant; its

[20] With the exception of Bardhan [8] and Mishan [67].

interpretation in the "interspatial" case is that prices are the same on account of free trade between the two countries. This seems to be a useful way of analyzing the implications of international differences in production functions.

Let us first analyze the case in which the isolated economy experiences technical progress at constant commodity prices in the labor intensive industry m, and no progress at all in industry c. In Figure 1.3, c_I and m_I are the isoquants for producing one unit of commodity

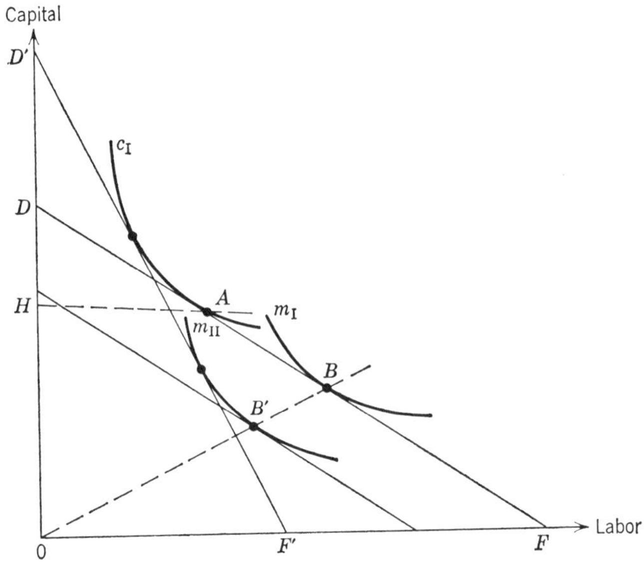

Figure 1.3

c and m, respectively (since commodity prices are constant, without loss of generality we can take prices to be unity so that the two unit isoquants have a common tangent at equilibrium); the slope of DF indicates the initial wage-rental ratio; A and B are the initial equilibrium points. Let us for the time being assume that technical progress is Hicks-neutral. So with factor-neutral technical improvement in industry m, the unit isoquant of m shifts toward the origin along $OB'B$ at the initial factor-price ratio. If commodity prices are to be kept constant, however, factor prices will have to be changed. The new factor-price ratio is given by the slope of $D'F'$.

Thus, with neutral technical progress in the more labor-intensive industry m, with no improvement in industry c, and with commodity prices kept constant, the wage-rentals ratio goes up.

What about the absolute level of factor prices? In the initial equilibrium, OD represents the cost of producing c or m in terms of capital, so that the reciprocal of the distance OD indicates the rental rate on capital R. Similarly, in initial equilibrium the reciprocal of OF represents the wage rate. In the new equilibrium the wage rate has gone up (with $1/OF' > 1/OF$) and the rental rate on capital has gone down (with $1/OD' < 1/OD$).

Let us now take the more general case in which Hicks-neutral technical progress occurs in both industries, but at a higher rate in the more labor-intensive industry m. In Figure 1.4a both the unit isoquants move toward the origin along given rays at the initial factor-price ratio, but that of m moves more than that of c. It is obvious from Figure 1.4a that if commodity prices are kept constant, both the wage-rental ratio (indicated by the slope of $D'F'$) and the absolute wage rate (the reciprocal of OF') will now be higher. What about the absolute rentals rate? It may actually go up (see Figure 1.4b), or down (Figure 1.4a), or remain the same (Figure 1.4c). From a comparison of Figures 1.4a, 1.4b, and 1.4c, it is apparent that R tends to go down the smaller the rate of technical progress in the more capital-intensive industry c, given the rate of technical progress in the

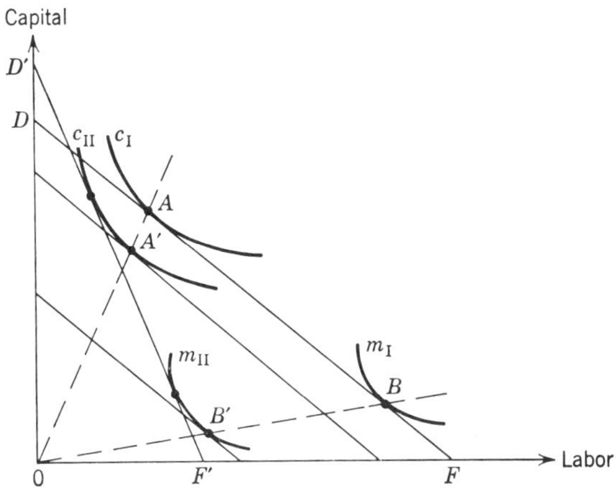

Figure 1.4a

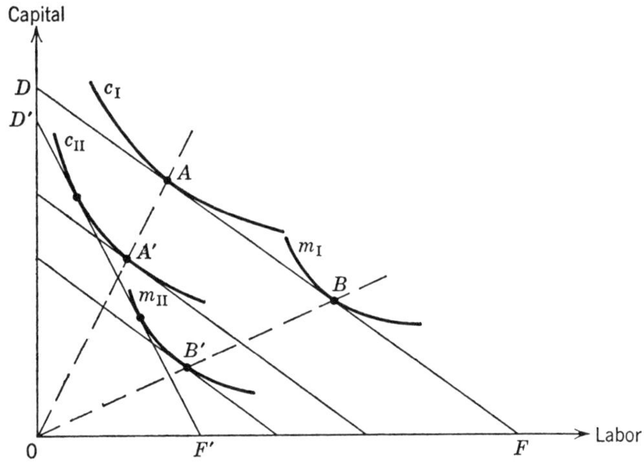

Figure 1.4b

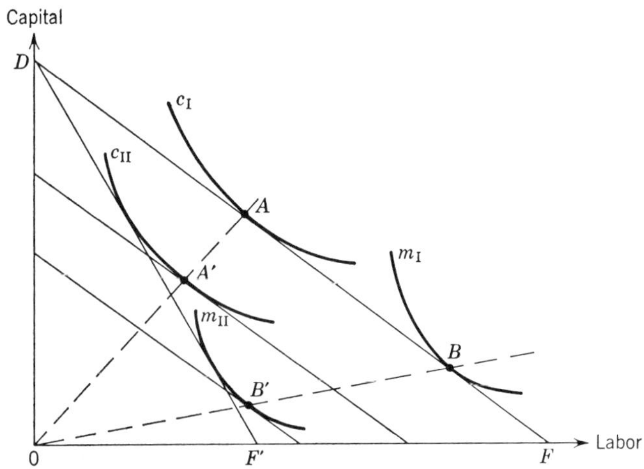

Figure 1.4c

labor-intensive industry m.[21] Thus, with a higher rate of technical progress in the labor-intensive industry and with commodity prices kept constant, both the absolute and relative wage rates go up, and if the *relative* rate of technical progress in the more labor-intensive industry is sufficiently high, the rental rate may remain the same or may even go down.

The third case we consider is one in which technical progress occurs in both industries at the same rate. From Figure 1.5 it is obvious that commodity prices as well as the wage-rentals ratio

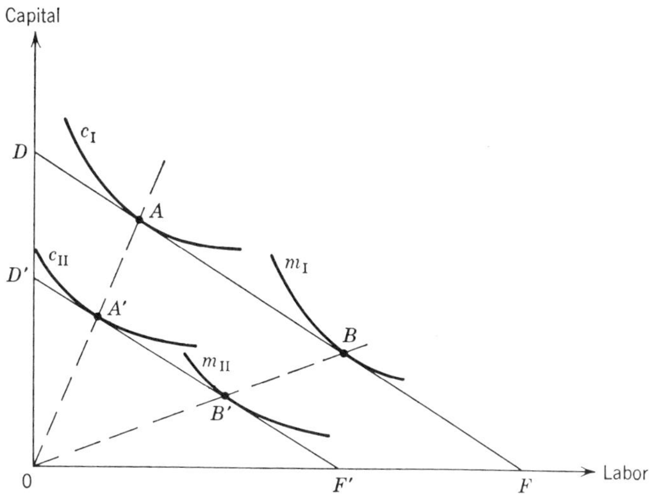

Figure 1.5

[21] More precisely it can be shown that R will go down, remain unchanged, or go up as λ_c/λ_m is less than, equal to, or greater than Q_c/Q_m, where λ_i is the rate of technical progress and Q_i the wage share in the ith industry. For a detailed proof, see Bardhan [8], p. 84. Hints of the proof: With neutral technical progress, (11) is changed to

$$P = \frac{f_c'[k_c(w)]e^{\lambda ct}}{f_m'[k_m(w)]e^{\lambda mt}}$$

and corresponding to (6) we shall now have

$$R = e^{\lambda ct}f_c'[k_c(w)].$$

Now keep P constant and take logarithmic derivatives of R with respect to t, using (9) and (10).

remain the same. As for absolute factor prices, both the wage rate and the rental rate go up.

For the remaining case, in which technical progress occurs at a higher rate in the more capital-intensive industry *c*, we can show by a similar diagrammatic analysis that with constant commodity prices the absolute and relative rental rate on capital goes up and the wage rate may remain the same or even go down if the *relative* rate of technical progress in the more capital-intensive industry is sufficiently high (the wage rate will certainly go down if there is no technical progress in the labor-intensive industry *m*).

So far we have considered only "neutral" technical progress at constant commodity prices. Introducing factor-biased technical change in this model is surprisingly easy, however, and does not alter any of the results[22] regarding factor prices, as long as the bias in technical progress does not reverse the original factor intensities, that is, *m* remains the more labor-intensive good compared with *c*. The intuitive idea behind this apparently surprising result is as follows. Factor-biased technical progress in an industry has often been looked upon as the joint operation of a neutral technical improvement *plus* a notional "saving" of a particular factor. In the case of labor (capital)-saving technical progress, we often say that it has the same effect as neutral technical progress combined with that of a notional increase in the supply of labor (capital). Now we know from the usual proof of a unique relationship between commodity and factor prices that a change in the supply of factors does not as such change (under the assumptions of the model) the factor prices as long as commodity prices remain the same. This is the basic reason why we find that factor-biased technical change has the same effect on factor prices as neutral technical change at the same commodity prices.

[22] For an algebraic proof of this result, take the equations in Bardhan [8], that pertain to the factor-neutral case, and add to them two equations, one indicating that the overall rate of technical progress in an industry is the weighted average of the rates at which the marginal products of the two factors rise on account of technical progress, the weights being the respective factor income shares in the industry and the other equation indicating that the bias of technical progress in the *i*th industry is equal to the difference between the rates at which marginal products of the two factors change on account of technical progress. It then turns out that the equations for rate of change of P, R, and W remain the same as before.

We now turn our analysis of technical progress at constant commodity prices into that of international differences in production functions with the same international prices established by free trade. We now have two countries, country *A* (technically the more advanced country) and country *B* (the backward country, our base of comparison). If, for example, in our former analysis there was a technical improvement in industry *c* and no change in industry *m*, this now means that the advanced country *A* is more efficient in producing *c* than the backward country *B* and as efficient in producing *m*. We can interpret all the other cases considered above in similar ways. In the diagrams drawn so far, for each commodity the outer unit isoquant can now be interpreted as belonging to the backward country and the inner unit isoquant as belonging to the advanced country. And whenever in our earlier analysis commodity prices were kept constant, this now means that the world prices are the same for both the countries under free international trade. We can now restate our conclusions from above in terms of the new model.

(a) If the advanced country is relatively more efficient in the labor-intensive commodity, both the relative and absolute wage rate will be higher there under free trade than in the backward country; if the advanced country's relative efficiency advantage in the labor-intensive industry is sufficiently high, the absolute rental rate may be the same or even lower in the advanced country than in the backward country.

(b) If the advanced country is more efficient than the other country in both industries to the same degree, the wage-rentals ratio will be the same in both the countries under free international trade. We thus have a case of *relative* factor price equalization. The absolute wage rate as well as the absolute rental rate will be higher in the advanced country, however.

(c) If the advanced country is relatively more efficient in producing the capital-intensive commodity, both the absolute and the relative rental rate on capital will be higher in the advanced country under free trade; if the advanced country's relative efficiency advantage in the capital-intensive industry is sufficiently high, the wage rate may the same or even lower in the advanced country.

These three propositions summarize our basic results regarding the factor-price pattern under free trade with international differences in production functions. In no case is the Heckscher–Samuelson result of complete equalization of *both* the factor prices obtained. In case (b) we obtain possible equalization of only the rental rate on capital, and in case (c) possible equalization of only the wage rate. None of these results depends on the relative factor endowment position of the two countries. Similarly, they do not depend on whether the efficiency advantage of the advanced country is more "biased" toward the use of one factor rather than another or is factor-neutral.[23]

There is not much systematic empirical knowledge available on the question of relative efficiency differences between countries. One can refer to the brief study made by Arrow et al. [4] in which they find "some slight indications, in comparing Japan and the United States, that the American advantage in efficiency tends to be least in capital-intensive industries."[24] Put in terms of our two-sector model and with the United States as the advanced country, this empirical information, for what it is worth, implies that the United States will have a *higher* wage rate than Japan under free trade; and if the American relative efficiency advantage in the more capital-intensive industry is small enough, the rental rate on capital in the United States will be *lower* than in Japan. This follows straight from our conclusion in case (a), and is a result probably not incompatible with reality.

Minhas [66], pp. 85–91, has made an empirical estimate of the percentage rates of return on capital in manufacturing sectors of a number of countries. His finding of relatively inconspicuous differences in the rates of returns on capital (which are approximately 19–20% in India and Japan, and 15–16% in Canada, the United Kingdom, and the United States) leads him to conclude:

"The over-all average rate of return on industrial capital appears to differ only slightly between the rich and poor countries. This result offers a serious challenge to many *a priori* notions which seem to be held on this subject."

[23] In comparing Japan with the United States, Arrow et al. [4] observe that the hypothesis of intercountry differences in the efficiency of factor use being factor-neutral stands up quite well in their statistical tests.

[24] A roughly similar result is obtained by Diaz-Alejandro [28] in his comparison of American and Argentine industries, and by Clague [27] in his comparison of American and Peruvian industries.

Let us take Minhas' empirical finding at its face value and try to interpret it in terms of our model. From our results above, we know that if of the two countries the more advanced country has a high enough relative efficiency advantage in the more labor-intensive industry, then and then alone, on our model, can the rental rate on capital in the advanced country be equal to (or even smaller than) that in the backward country under free trade. Minhas [66] p. 90, tries to give the following explanation of his findings:

"The realisation of relatively low rates of return on industrial capital in the poor countries in spite of extremely low-capital-labor ratios is most likely due to low levels of efficiency in the use of factors of production."

If it is at all useful to explain this phenomenon in terms of our two-sector model with free trade, it can be said that it is *not enough* to attribute it to relatively "low levels of efficiency in the use of factors of production" in poor, backward countries. As we have seen above, we have to specify a particular pattern of relative efficiency disadvantage in the backward country to explain the phenomenon in terms of our model. If, for example, the backward country is less efficient than the advanced country in both industries to the same degree, it can be seen from our case (b) that Minhas' finding is not corroborated by our model.[25]

Let us add some final comments on some of the broad features of our model.

(i) We have implicitly assumed throughout that the "advanced" country is technically at least as advanced as the other country in any given industry. This seems to exclude the case in which one country is more efficient in one industry and *less* efficient in the other industry than the other country. Although we have not explicitly considered this case, it can be easily handled in terms of the techniques of analysis we have employed.

(ii) It might seem that in our model production functions differ internationally only on the basis of technical knowledge being

[25] The relative similarity of rates of return on capital in different countries might be, in part, explained by international movements of capital (which are ruled out in our model). This is a point of doubtful importance in this context in view of the relatively small amount of capital that flows from rich to poor countries, however.

different in the two countries. However, technical efficiency in our model is a "dummy" capable of representing any kind of shifting parameter that is introduced. Thus, intercountry parametric variations (say, in Taussig's "climate" or Meade's "atmosphere") in production functions may easily be taken care of in terms of our model.

(iii) In our model international differences in production functions are assumed to be such that the isoquant for one country lies totally outside that of the other country: They do not intersect. This means that for the commodity concerned, one country is unambiguously more efficient than the other.

2

ECONOMIC GROWTH AND PATTERNS OF INTERNATIONAL SPECIALIZATION

2.1. SUFFICIENT CONDITIONS FOR INCOMPLETE SPECIALIZATION

In this chapter we briefly consider how economic growth affects the pattern of international specialization in terms of the basic model set up in Chapter 1. In particular, most of this chapter is devoted to the question of how the relative factor endowment positions (and shifts in them) of the two countries determine whether a country is completely or incompletely specialized. We continue to assume that of the two goods m is always the more labor-intensive (as before, the opposite factor intensity case can be analyzed similarly). For simplicity, we start with the assumption, shortly to be relaxed, that production functions are internationally identical as in the Heckscher–Ohlin–Samuelson model.

Let us take Figure 1.1 and redraw it as Figure 2.1.[1] Suppose the

[1] As the production functions are internationally identical, the curves hold good for both countries, although we have used notations for one country only.

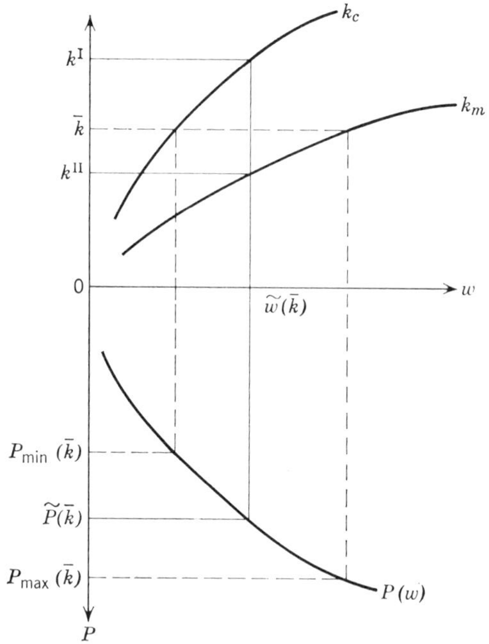

Figure 2.1

capital-labor ratio ($\bar{k}$) for the foreign country as a whole is given, then the comparative cost range is the gap between what we have called $P_{\min}(\bar{k})$ and $P_{\max}(\bar{k})$.

With nonreversal of factor intensities, concave homogeneous production functions, and freely mobile factors, the production-possibility curve relating output of m with output of c is strictly concave[2] to the origin. With a convex aggregate preference set this implies that given the capital-labor ratio $\bar{k}$ for the foreign country, there is a unique *closed-economy* equilibrium relative price of m, $\tilde{P}(\bar{k})$, for the foreign country and hence a unique *closed-economy* equilibrium wage-rentals ratio $\tilde{w}(\bar{k})$. Barring the case of perverse demand conditions (such as wage-earners strongly preferring the labor-intensive good, and so on), the larger the capital-labor ratio

[2] For sufficient conditions for a strictly concave (inward) transformation surface in the case in which there are more than two goods and two factors, see Lancaster [59], p. 134.

of the foreign country, the higher its closed-economy equilibrium wage-rentals ratio, so that $\tilde{w}'(\bar{k}) > 0$.

Now, given $\bar{k}$, we want first to determine the range of values of k, the capital-labor ratio in the home country, through which the country must be incompletely specialized. We know that if one country's comparative cost range includes the other country's closed-economy equilibrium price ratio, the former country will not specialize.[3] This is because in this case both countries' closed-economy equilibrium price ratios and hence the free-trade world price will be within the former country's comparative cost range. Given $\tilde{P}(\bar{k})$, the closed-economy equilibrium price ratio for the foreign country, it is easy to see from Figure 2.1 that it will be included in the comparative cost range of the home country if the latter's capital-labor ratio k is below (or equal to) k^I and above (or equal to) k^{II}. Thus, given $\bar{k}$, the home country must be incompletely specialized as long as $k^I \geq k \geq k^{II}$. For different values of $\bar{k}$, we can in this way define the range of k for which the home country must be incompletely specialized.

Since $\tilde{w}'(\bar{k}) > 0$, both k^I and k^{II} are increasing functions of $\bar{k}$. In other words, as $\bar{k}$ increases, the limiting values of k *sufficient* for the home country to be incompletely specialized also increases. Figure 2.2 incorporates the above argument. The region between the curves a and b is the region in which the home country must be incompletely specialized. The exact shape of these two curves (apart from the fact that they will be upward-sloping and nonintersecting except at the origin) will depend on the elasticities of substitution

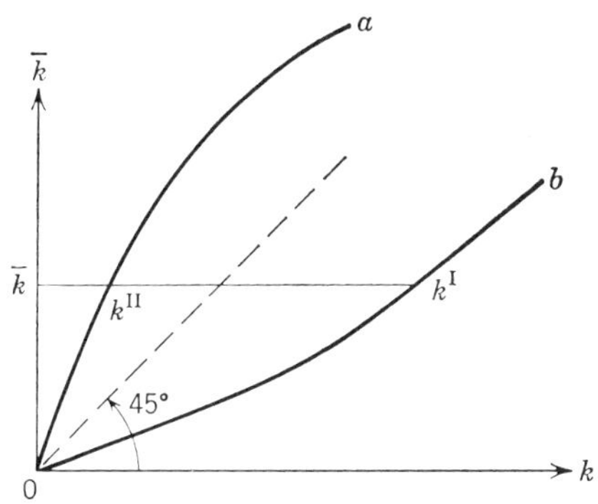

Figure 2.2

[3] See Johnson [49], p. 23.

and the difference in factor intensities between the two sectors. One important point to note is that being located in the region between curves *a* and *b* is a sufficient condition for the home country to be incompletely specialized but certainly not a necessary condition.

The assumption of internationally identical production functions can now easily be relaxed. Figure 2.1 is now to be replaced by Figure 2.3. For simplicity, we assume that the efficiency advantage of the technically more advanced home country is "factor-neutral," so that the k_c and k_m curves in the upper quadrant of Figure 2.3 are the same for both countries.[4] We also assume (the opposite case is

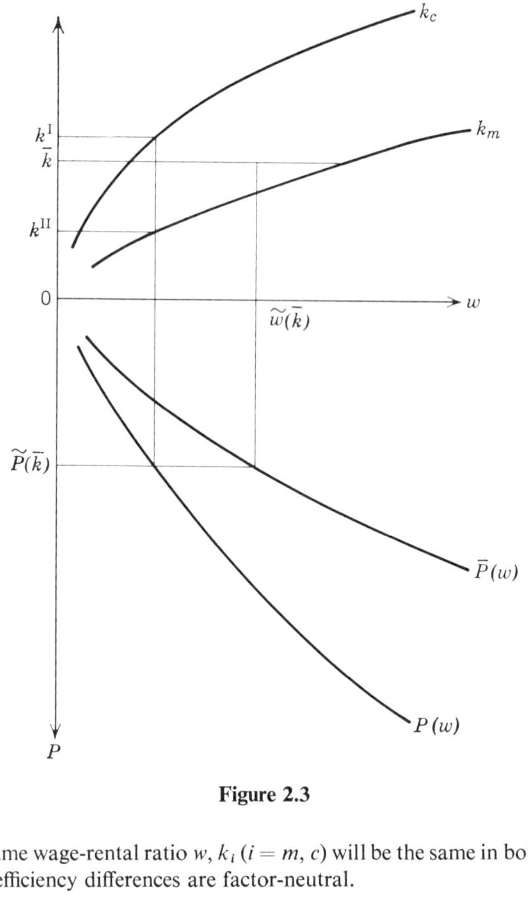

Figure 2.3

[4] For the same wage-rental ratio w, k_i ($i = m, c$) will be the same in both countries as long as efficiency differences are factor-neutral.

analogous) that the home country is relatively more efficient in the more capital-intensive commodity c, so that the curve relating the wage-rentals ratio w to the price ratio P, $P(w)$ for the home country, is below the corresponding curve for the foreign country $\bar{P}(w)$.[5]

Now, given $\bar{k}$, the capital-labor ratio of the foreign country, a *unique* closed-economy equilibrium price ratio $\tilde{P}(\bar{k})$ exists as before, provided the production-possibility curve is strictly concave to the origin and the aggregate preference set is convex. Given this, we want to determine, as before, the range of values of k, the capital-labor ratio of the home country, for which it must be incompletely specialized. As before, we know that if one country's comparative cost range includes the other country's closed-economy equilibrium price ratio, the former country will *not* specialize completely. From Figure 2.3, it is obvious that $\tilde{P}(\bar{k})$ will be included in the comparative cost range of the home country if its capital-labor ratio k is below (or equal to) k^I and above (or equal to) k^{II}. Thus, given $\bar{k}$, the home country must be incompletely specialized as long as $k^I \geq k \geq k^{II}$ in Figure 2.3. It is also easy to confirm, as before, that both k^I and k^{II} are increasing functions of $\bar{k}$.

2.2. NECESSARY AND SUFFICIENT CONDITIONS FOR COMPLETE SPECIALIZATION

In Section 2.1 we derived *sufficient* conditions for *incomplete specialization* in the home country as the capital-labor ratio in the foreign country changes. In this section we go farther and with the help of extra assumptions try to determine the *necessary and sufficient* conditions for *complete specialization* in each commodity in the home country.[6]

In Section 1.1 we noted that under usual demand assumptions demand for imports of m is a declining function of the relative price of m, so that $\partial Z_m/\partial P < 0$ and $\partial Z_m/\partial P < 0$.

From (17) of Chapter 1, in equilibrium

$$z_m + \bar{z}_m \gamma = 0, \tag{1}$$

[5] For the same wage-rentals ratio w, P will be higher for the country with the higher *relative* efficiency advantage in good c.

[6] The analysis in this section is a generalization of that presented by Oniki and Uzawa [72]. For the case in which demand depends on distribution of income, see Bardhan [9].

where z_m and $\bar{z}_m$ are per capita demands for imports of m in the home and foreign countries, respectively, and $\gamma = \bar{L}/L$ is the ratio of the labor force in the two countries. For the discussion in this section let us, for simplification, assume that the labor supplies in the two countries are given so that γ is a constant (in fact the results hold if we allow the labor force to grow at the same rate in both countries, which keeps γ constant), and the only source of growth is capital accumulation. Equation (1) then uniquely determines the equilibrium world price $P(k, \bar{k})$ as shown in Figure 2.4.

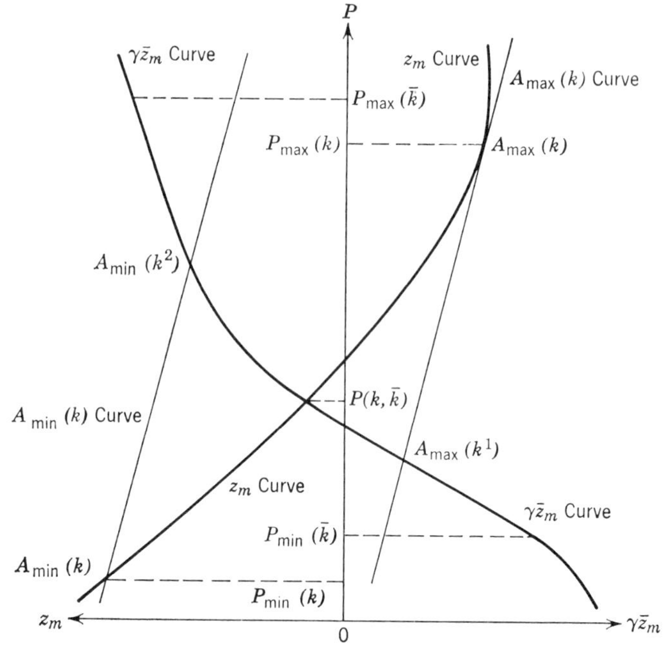

Figure 2.4

In Figure 2.4 the z_m curve representing per capita demand for imports of m in the home country is drawn in the left-hand quadrant. When the z_m curve crosses into the right-hand quadrant, z_m becomes negative, that is, m now tends to be *exported* by the home country. The same applies to the $\gamma\bar{z}_m$ curve drawn in the right-hand quadrant; when the $\gamma\bar{z}_m$ curve crosses into the left-hand quadrant, m tends to be *exported* by the foreign country. The intersection of the z_m curve and the $\gamma\bar{z}_m$ curve gives us the equilibrium price $P(k, \bar{k})$.

Let us define

$$A_{\max}(k) = -z_m[P_{\max}(k), k]$$

and

$$A_{\min}(k) = -z_m[P_{\min}(k), k].$$

This means that $A_{\max}(k)$ is the amount of per capita supply of *exports* of m by the home country when the world price $P = P_{\max}(k)$, that is, when the home country has just gone into complete specialization in production of m; and $A_{\min}(k)$ is the amount of per capita demand for imports of m by the home country when the world price $P = P_{\min}(k)$, that is, when the home country is completely specialized in producing c but just on the border line. As k increases from zero to infinity, $A_{\max}(k)$ and $A_{\min}(k)$ both describe continuous curves on $(P, \gamma\bar{z}_m)$ and (P, z_m) planes.

In Figure 2.4 the $A_{\max}$ curve is the locus of all $A_{\max}$ points on the z_m curves, that is, it is the locus of all the points on the z_m curves (corresponding to different k values) from which points "onward" the home country is completely specialized in m. The $A_{\min}$ curve is, similarly the locus of all $A_{\min}$ points on the z_m curves, that is, it is the locus of all the points on z_m curves (corresponding to different k values) "up to" which the home country is completely specialized in good c. How do we determine the shapes of these curves?

Let us call s the proportion of per capita national income spent on m. When income and price elasticity of demand for m is unity, this proportion is constant (the only case considered by Oniki and Uzawa [72] in their analysis of specialization). In general s will depend on relative price P and per capita income y, so that the per capita demand for m is

$$\frac{D_m}{L} = s(P, y)\frac{y}{P}. \tag{2}$$

From (2), price elasticity of per capita demand for m (positively defined) is

$$\varepsilon = 1 - \frac{\partial s}{\partial P}\frac{P}{s}$$

and income elasticity of per capita demand for m is

$$e = 1 + \frac{\partial s}{\partial y}\frac{y}{s}.$$

When the country is completely specialized in the production of m, $y = Pf_m$ and per capita demand for imports of m is $-(1-s)f_m$, so that

$$A_{\max}(k) = [1 - s(P_{\max}(k), y(P_{\max}(k), k))]f_m(k). \tag{3}$$

It is easily seen that

$$\frac{dA_{\max}}{dk} = (1 - es)f'_m + (\varepsilon - e)\frac{sf_m}{P}\frac{dP_{\max}}{dk}. \tag{4}$$

Since $dP_{\max}/dk > 0$ (which is obvious from Figure 1.1), $dA_{\max}/dk > 0$ under the sufficient conditions of

$$\text{(a) } \varepsilon \geq e \qquad \text{and} \qquad \text{(b) } 1 \geq e.$$

Under these conditions the $A_{\max}(k)$ curve is of the shape shown in Figure 2.4. Oniki and Uzawa [72] found the same shape for the $A_{\max}(k)$ curve, but their condition $\varepsilon = e = 1$ is only a special case of the general condition.

Given the shape of the $\gamma\bar{z}_m$ curve (for any given $\bar{k}$) and of the $A_{\max}(k)$ curve as in Figure 2.4, we can see that these two curves will intersect only once. Let k^1 be the capital-labor ratio of the home country, corresponding to the intersection point (for a given $\bar{k}$). It is easy to confirm that the home country is completely specialized in m *if and only if* k does not exceed k^1 for a given $\bar{k}$. With an increase in $\bar{k}$, the capital-labor ratio of the foreign country, this critical ratio k^1 will increase only if the $\gamma\bar{z}_m$ curve shifts upward with increasing $\bar{k}$ and given P, that is, if

$$\frac{\partial \bar{z}_m(P, \bar{k})}{\partial \bar{k}} > 0.$$

Let us find out if this is true.

As long as the $\gamma\bar{z}_m$ curve is in the right-hand quadrant of Figure 2.4, the foreign country is either incompletely specialized or completely specialized in good c. In the first case, that is, when the foreign country is incompletely specialized, per capita demand for imports of m is

$$\bar{z}_m = \frac{\bar{D}_m}{\bar{L}}(P, \bar{y}) - \bar{f}_m(\bar{k}_m)\frac{(\bar{k}_c - \bar{k})}{\bar{k}_c - \bar{k}_m}, \tag{5}$$

where we have used (2), (14), and (23) of Chapter 1. Since $\bar{y} = \bar{W} + \bar{R}\bar{k}$, where $\bar{W}$ is the wage rate and $\bar{R}$ the rental rate in the foreign country, it is clear that with positive marginal propensity to spend on m and with m as the labor-intensive good,

$$\frac{\partial \bar{z}_m(P, \bar{k})}{\partial \bar{k}} > 0. \tag{6}$$

In the second case, in which the foreign country is completely specialized in production of c,

$$\bar{z}_m = \frac{\bar{D}_m}{\bar{L}}(P, \bar{y}), \tag{7}$$

where $\bar{y} = \bar{f}_c(\bar{k})$.

Once again, with positive marginal propensity to spend on m,

$$\frac{\partial \bar{z}_m(P, \bar{k})}{\partial \bar{k}} > 0. \tag{8}$$

So we can now say that k^1 goes up as the capital-labor ratio of the foreign country goes up. In Figure 2.5 the home country is completely specialized in m *if and only if* the relative factor endowment ratio is

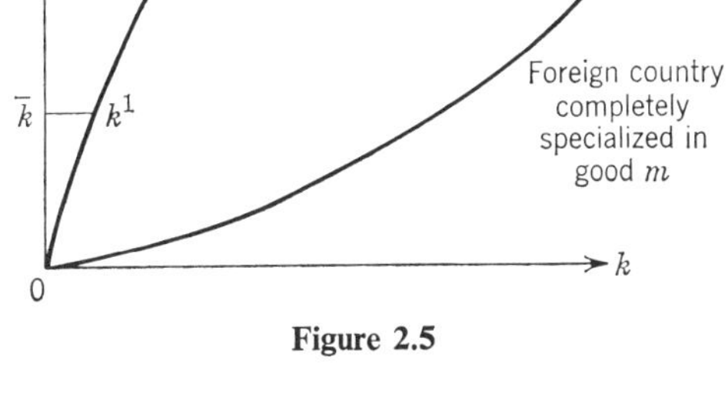

Figure 2.5

in the region bordered by the $\bar{k}$ axis and curve c. Carrying out a similar analysis for the foreign country, we can find that under similar conditions the foreign country is completely specialized in m *if and only if* the relative factor-endowment ratio is in the region bordered by the k axis and curve $\bar{c}$.

It is more difficult to obtain a monotonic shape for the $A_{\min}(k)$ curve. When the home country is completely specialized in production of c, $y = f_c(k)$ and

$$A_{\min}(k) = s[P_{\min}(k), y(k)] \frac{f_c(k)}{P_{\min}(k)}. \tag{9}$$

It is easy to see that

$$\frac{dA_{\min}(k)}{dk} = eP_{\min}(k)f_c'(k) - \varepsilon f_c(k) \frac{dP_{\min}(k)}{dk}. \tag{10}$$

Since from Figure 1.1,

$$\frac{dP_{\min}(k)}{dk} > 0,$$

it is difficult to be unambiguous about the sign of (10). From that Figure, however, it is clear that the smaller the elasticity of factor substitution,

$$\sigma_c = \frac{dk_c}{dw} \frac{w}{k_c},$$

in industry c, the larger the value of

$$\frac{dP_{\min}(k)}{dk},$$

and so if σ_c is small enough and if $\varepsilon \geq e$,

$$\frac{dA_{\min}(k)}{dk} < 0$$

and we have an $A_{\min}(k)$ curve of the shape shown in Figure 2.4.

Given the shapes of the $\gamma\bar{z}_m$ curve[7] (for any given $\bar{k}$) and of the $A_{\min}(k)$ curve, the only intersection point between these two curves gives us a corresponding capital-labor ratio k^2 for the home country. Given $\bar{k}$, the home country is completely specialized in good c if k

[7] Note that if $\bar{s}$ is constant, the $\gamma\bar{z}_m$ curve is a vertical line for $P > P_{\max}(\bar{k})$.

does not fall below k^2. Now as the capital-labor ratio in the foreign country $\bar{k}$ goes up, this critical ratio k^2 will increase only if the $\gamma\bar{z}_m$ curve shifts upward with increasing $\bar{k}$ and given P, that is,

$$\frac{\partial \bar{z}_m(P, \bar{k})}{\partial \bar{k}} > 0.$$

As long as the $\gamma\bar{z}_m$ curve is in the left-hand quadrant of Figure 2.4, the foreign country is either incompletely specialized or completely specialized in good m. In the former case,

$$\frac{\partial \bar{z}_m(P, \bar{k})}{\partial \bar{k}} < 0,$$

as we have seen in (6). In the second case, when the foreign country is completely specialized in m,

$$\bar{z}_m = -\{1 - \bar{s}[P, \bar{y}(\bar{k})]\}\bar{f}_m(\bar{k}), \tag{11}$$

where

$$\bar{y}(\bar{k}) = P\bar{f}_m(\bar{k}).$$

It is easy to see that

$$\frac{\partial \bar{z}_m(P, \bar{k})}{\partial \bar{k}} > 0, \qquad \text{if and only if} \qquad \bar{e} > \frac{1}{\bar{s}} > 1, \tag{12}$$

where $\bar{e}$ is the income elasticity of demand for m in the foreign country.

Under condition (12), k^2 is an increasing function of $\bar{k}$, and the home country is completely specialized in good c *if and only if* the relative factor endowment ratio is in the region bordered by the k axis and curve d in Figure 2.6.

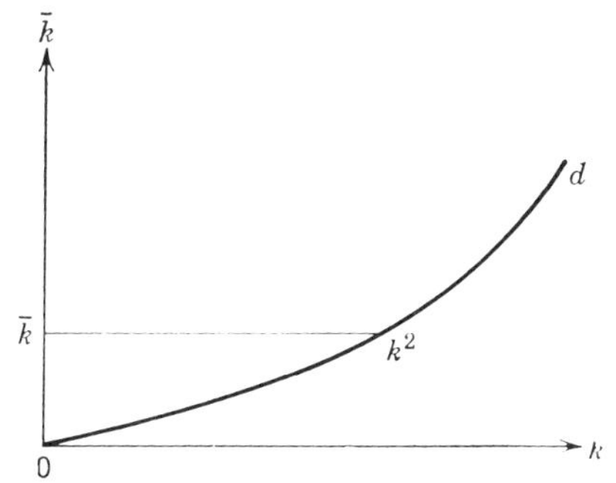

Figure 2.6

2.3. TECHNICAL PROGRESS AND SPECIALIZATION

In this section we consider the question of technical progress and the pattern of specialization. On the one hand, technical progress, through its sheer effect on technology, affects P_{max} and P_{min} and thus the comparative cost range of a country; on the other hand, through its effects on income and demand as well as effects on costs, it affects the world price. Since a country's pattern of specialization is determined by a comparison of the world price P with its comparative cost range bordered by P_{max} and P_{min}, technical progress obviously can alter the specialization pattern. A number of tedious alternative cases could be analyzed here, but we shall confine ourselves to one simple illustration.

Suppose the home country is small enough not to be able to affect the world price P. Now let us suppose that neutral technical progress occurs in both industries and the foreign price remains the same. Going back to Figure 1.1, the k_c and k_m curves remain as before because of the factor neutrality of technical improvement; the $P(w)$ curve in the lower quadrant will shift down, up, or remain the same as the rate of technical progress increases, decreases, or remains the same in industry c compared to industry m. If, for example, technical progress occurs at a higher rate in industry c, both P_{max} and P_{min} will be higher. If this goes on for some time, P_{min} will tend to exceed the given world price P and the home country will tend to be completely specialized, which is an intuitively obvious result.

By using more involved calculations for the demand and cost effects of technical progress in more complicated cases, less self-evident results can be derived. Let us mention one such result without proof. If there is neutral or capital-saving technical progress in the capital-intensive industry c, the foreign country is static (or at least the foreign country's industry c is improving at a slower rate), the home country spends a constant proportion of its national income on m (this assumption may easily be relaxed), and if m is not a Giffen good in the foreign country, then the home country will be driven toward complete specialization in c and the static foreign country toward complete specialization in m.

3

EQUILIBRIUM GROWTH WITH TRADE IN CONSUMER AND CAPITAL GOODS

3.1. A SIMPLE DYNAMIC MODEL

In the preceding chapters we considered growth to be "exogenous"; given particular patterns of growth, we worked out their comparative-static implications. We now want to turn our model into a continuous and endogenous accumulation model.[1] Good c is redefined as a homogeneous consumer good and good m as a homogeneous capital good. The demand function for good m now gives us the savings function for the economy. For easier handling of the model in this chapter we take a particular case of the demand condition described in earlier chapters. We assume that a constant proportion s of national income is saved and invested. Our purpose is to study some of the properties of dynamic equilibrium in terms of such a model. The model is basically the same as that used in the recent

[1] Since (uniform) Harrod-neutral technical progress in the two sectors in effect is labor-augmenting and introduces problems akin to those of growth in labor supply, it can easily be introduced into the model.

spurt of two-sector neoclassical growth models in which international trade has, however, been generally ignored.[2]

Consumption goods are instantaneously consumed and capital goods are accumulated as capital stock. We shall assume that capital is "immortal" (depreciation at a fixed percentage rate can be very easily introduced without affecting the essential results). The rate of capital accumulation is thus determined by the amount of domestic output and imports of capital goods:

$$\dot{K} = F_m + Z_m. \tag{1}$$

Let us also assume that labor grows at a constant positive rate μ, so that

$$\dot{L} = \mu L. \tag{2}$$

From the savings behavior assumed and from (1) and (2), the rate of growth of the capital-labor ratio k is

$$\frac{\dot{k}}{k} = \frac{\dot{K}}{K} - \frac{\dot{L}}{L} = \frac{sy}{Pk} - \mu, \tag{3}$$

where y $(= w + Rk)$ is the per capita national income. As the equations for the foreign country are the same with only overbars denoting the foreign country,

$$\frac{\dot{\bar{k}}}{\bar{k}} = \frac{\dot{\bar{K}}}{\bar{K}} - \frac{\dot{\bar{L}}}{\bar{L}} = \frac{\overline{sy}}{P\bar{k}} - \bar{\mu}. \tag{4}$$

Let us now note some of the characteristics of the steady state in this international economy. In the steady state, capital and labor grow at the same rate (μ for the home country and $\bar{\mu}$ for the foreign country); national income, value of exports, value of imports, and so on, all grow at this rate. We can write the steady-state rate of growth of imports of capital goods $\dot{Z}_m/Z_m = \mu$ and $\dot{\bar{Z}}_m/\bar{Z}_m = \bar{\mu}$.[3] Now

[2] Our analysis in this chapter closely follows that of Oniki and Uzawa [72], but we dispense with their assumption of internationally identical production functions. For an alternative trade model, in which none of the wage income and part or all of the rental income is saved, equilibrium growth is analyzed in Bardhan [11]. The results for this classical savings case, when they differ from the proportional savings case, will be mentioned in the footnotes in this chapter.

[3] In the steady state P is constant, so that the *value* of imports of capital goods grows at the same rate as their quantity.

from the international equilibrium condition of (17) in Chapter 1,

$$Z_m + \bar{Z}_m = 0. \tag{5}$$

Therefore, $\dot{Z}_m/Z_m$ and $\dot{\bar{Z}}_m/\bar{Z}_m$ should be equal, which means that in this model unless the two trading countries have the same natural rates of growth there can be no steady state. This is certainly a serious limitation of the relevance of the steady-state analysis in terms of such a model. This limitation, however, has no connection with the neoclassical aspects of the model; it follows only from our assumptions of constant rate of growth of labor and the absence of foreign lending or borrowing. We shall in this chapter[4] assume that $\mu = \bar{\mu}$. It is interesting to note that if both countries are incompletely specialized and if production functions are internationally identical, it follows[5] from (3) and (4) that in the steady state $k/\bar{k} = s/\bar{s}$, that is, the capital-labor ratios of the two countries are in the same proportion as their saving rates.

The per capita demand for imports of capital goods in the home country is

$$z_m(P, k) = \frac{sf_c(k)}{P}, \tag{6}$$

when the country is completely specialized in producing consumer goods,

$$z_m(k) = -(1 - s)f_m(k), \tag{7}$$

when the country is completely specialized in producing capital goods, or

$$z_m(P, k) = \frac{sy}{P} - f_m(k_m)\frac{(k_c - k)}{k_c - k_m}, \tag{8}$$

when the country is incompletely specialized.

From (23) of Chapter 1, we have substituted for L_m/L. Per capita

[4] For an analysis of a case in which the foreign rate of growth is different from the domestic rate, see Chapter 4.

[5] This is true because under those assumptions $w = \bar{w}$ and $R = \bar{R}$ (on account of factor-price equalization) and because $y = w + Rk$ and $\mu = \bar{\mu}$. In the case in which all of the wage income is consumed and a fraction s_r of rental income is saved, we must have $s_r = \bar{s}_r$ for both the countries to be in a steady state with incomplete specialization and internationally identical production functions.

national income $y = w + Rk$. From Section 1.1 it is now easy to see why in (8) z_m is a function of P and k alone.

Since we have assumed that $\mu = \bar{\mu}$, $\gamma = \bar{L}/L$ is again a constant, as in Chapter 2, and we can therefore use the equation

$$z_m(P, k) + \bar{z}_m(P, \bar{k})\gamma = 0 \tag{9}$$

to determine the equilibrium world price $P(k, \bar{k})$, as in Figure 2.4 of Chapter 2.[6]

From (9) we obtain, analogous to (19) of Chapter 1:

$$\frac{\partial P}{\partial k} = -\frac{\dfrac{\partial z_m}{\partial k}}{\left(\dfrac{\partial z_m}{\partial P} + \gamma\dfrac{\partial \bar{z}_m}{\partial P}\right)} \tag{10}$$

and

$$\frac{\partial P}{\partial \bar{k}} = -\frac{\dfrac{\partial \bar{z}_m}{\partial \bar{k}}}{\left(\dfrac{\partial z_m}{\partial P} + \gamma\dfrac{\partial \bar{z}_m}{\partial P}\right)}. \tag{11}$$

We have already seen that under usual well-behaved demand functions the denominator of the right-hand side of (10) and (11) is negative, that is, the stability condition of momentary international equilibrium of Chapter 1 is satisfied. The same is true of the special demand function in this chapter when a constant proportion of national income is spent on each good; with unit price and income elasticities of demand, the demand functions are particularly well-behaved.

If we continue to assume that capital goods are more labor-intensive in production, that is, $k_c > k_m$—the well-known capital-intensive condition of the literature on two-sector growth models—we obtain from (6), (7), and (8),

$$\frac{\partial z_m(P, k)}{\partial k} > 0, \tag{12}$$

[6] The only difference is in the vertical stretch of the z_m and $\bar{z}_m\gamma$ curves in the region of complete specialization in m. See footnote 7, Chapter 2.

when the home country is either completely specialized in c or incompletely specialized, and

$$\frac{\partial z_m(k)}{\partial k} < 0, \tag{13}$$

when the home country is completely specialized in m.

From (10), (11), (12), and (13) we know the following results concerning the effects of variations of k and $\bar{k}$ on P.

Case (a)

When both countries are incompletely specialized (henceforth we shall refer to this case as $[H(c, m); B(c, m)]$, H denoting the home country and B the foreign country):

$$\frac{\partial P}{\partial k} > 0, \qquad \frac{\partial P}{\partial \bar{k}} > 0. \tag{14}$$

Case (b)

When the home country is incompletely specialized and the foreign country is completely specialized in capital goods (henceforth we shall refer to this case as $[H(c, m); B(m)]$):

$$\frac{\partial P}{\partial k} > 0, \qquad \frac{\partial P}{\partial \bar{k}} < 0. \tag{15}$$

Case (c)

When the home country is incompletely specialized and the foreign country is completely specialized in consumer goods, that is, $[H(c, m); B(c)]$:

$$\frac{\partial P}{\partial k} > 0, \qquad \frac{\partial P}{\partial \bar{k}} > 0. \tag{16}$$

Case (d)

When the home country is completely specialized in capital goods and the foreign country in consumer goods, that is, $[H(m); B(c)]$:

$$\frac{\partial P}{\partial k} < 0, \qquad \frac{\partial P}{\partial \bar{k}} > 0. \tag{17}$$

The results for the other possible three patterns of specialization—$[H(m); B(c, m)]$, $[H(c); B(c, m)]$, and $[H(c); B(m)]$—can easily be inferred from the first four cases with suitable interchange of country denotations. In general, if a country is not specialized in capital goods, the relative world price of capital goods increases whenever the capital-labor ratio of that country increases; the relative world price of capital goods decreases with a rise in the capital-labor ratio of a country completely specialized in capital goods.

3.2. THE ACCUMULATION EQUATIONS

We are now ready to analyze the time path of capital accumulation in the two trading countries.

Case (a) $[H(c, m); B(c, m)]$

From (3) and (4), we can now write the differential equations governing capital accumulation.

$$\frac{\dot{k}}{k} = \frac{sy(P, k)}{Pk} - \mu = \phi(k, \bar{k}) \tag{18}$$

Since per capita national income $y = w + Rk$ in terms of factor payments and since factor prices with incomplete specialization are unique functions of P, we can write $y = y(P, k)$ and with P constant, $\partial y/\partial k = R = Pf'_m$. Since y is also the value of per capita total output, that is, $y = f_c l_c + Pf_m l_m$, where l_c and l_m are, as in Chapter 1, L_c/L and L_m/L, respectively, $\partial y/\partial P = f_m l_m$; this is because along the production-possibility curve $d(f_c l_c)/d(f_m l_m) = -P$.

So now,

$$\phi_k = -\frac{s}{P^2k^2}\left[P(y - Pf'_m k) + k\frac{\partial P}{\partial k}(y - Pf_m l_m)\right] < 0 \tag{19}$$

and

$$\phi_{\bar{k}} = -\frac{s}{P^2k}[y - Pf_m l_m]\frac{\partial P}{\partial \bar{k}} < 0. \tag{20}$$

Similarly, for the foreign country

$$\frac{\dot{\bar{k}}}{\bar{k}} = \frac{\overline{sy}(P, \bar{k})}{P\bar{k}} - \mu = \psi(k, \bar{k}) \tag{21}$$

and $\psi_{\bar{k}} < 0$, $\psi_k < 0$. It is also easy to confirm that $\phi_k/\phi_{\bar{k}} > \psi_k/\psi_{\bar{k}}$. All this means that[7]

$$\left(\frac{d\bar{k}}{dk}\right)_{\dot{k}=0} < \left(\frac{d\bar{k}}{dk}\right)_{\dot{\bar{k}}=0} < 0. \tag{22}$$

Case (b) $[H(c, m); B(m)]$

In this case, (18) is again valid, but from (15), (19), and (20), $\phi_k < 0$ and $\phi_{\bar{k}} > 0$, so that

$$\left(\frac{d\bar{k}}{dk}\right)_{\dot{k}=0} > 0. \tag{23}$$

The accumulation equation for the foreign country is now given by

$$\frac{\dot{\bar{k}}}{\bar{k}} = \frac{\bar{s}\bar{f}_m(\bar{k})}{\bar{k}} - \mu = \psi(\bar{k}) \tag{24}$$

and

$$\psi_{\bar{k}} < 0. \tag{25}$$

Case (c) $[H(c, m); B(c)]$

In this case, (18) is again valid, and from (16) it is easy to see that (19) and (20) are also valid. The accumulation equation for the foreign country is now given by

$$\frac{\dot{\bar{k}}}{\bar{k}} = \frac{\bar{s}\bar{f}_c(\bar{k})}{P\bar{k}} - \mu = \psi(k, \bar{k}). \tag{26}$$

[7] In the case in which instead of a proportional savings function we have a "classical" saving function for each country, (22) changes to

$$\left(\frac{d\bar{k}}{dk}\right)_{\dot{k}=0} = \left(\frac{d\bar{k}}{dk}\right)_{\dot{\bar{k}}=0} < 0.$$

It is easy to confirm that

$$\psi_k < 0, \psi_{\bar{k}} < 0 \qquad \text{and} \qquad \frac{\phi_k}{\phi_{\bar{k}}} > \frac{\psi_k}{\psi_{\bar{k}}}.$$

All this means[8] that as in (22) in this case also

$$\left(\frac{d\bar{k}}{dk}\right)_{\dot{k}=0} < \left(\frac{d\bar{k}}{dk}\right)_{\dot{\bar{k}}=0} < 0. \tag{27}$$

Case (d) $[H(m); B(c)]$

In this case

$$\frac{\dot{k}}{k} = \frac{sf_m(k)}{k} - \mu = \phi(k), \tag{28}$$

with

$$\phi_k < 0 \tag{29}$$

The accumulation equation for the foreign country is given by (26) and $\psi_k > 0$, $\psi_{\bar{k}} < 0$, so that[8]

$$\left(\frac{d\bar{k}}{dk}\right)_{\dot{\bar{k}}=0} > 0. \tag{30}$$

As mentioned before, for the other three patterns of specialization, similar conclusions (with suitable change of country denotations) hold.

3.3. STABILITY ANALYSIS

We have analyzed the shapes of $\dot{k} = 0$ and $\dot{\bar{k}} = 0$ curves for each pattern of international specialization. Let us now examine all of them together and find out what in general can be said about the existence, uniqueness, and global stability of growth equilibrium in the model. We are, of course, assuming throughout that the capital good is more labor-intensive in production.

[8] For the "classical" savings function case the extra assumption of high enough elasticity of factor substitution in consumer goods industry of the foreign country (say $\bar{\sigma}_c \geq 1$) is needed as a sufficient condition for (27) and (30) to be valid.

Taking Figure 2.5, and given the assumption that a constant proportion s of national income is spent on m, so that $\varepsilon = e = 1$, the home country is completely specialized in m *if and only if* the relative factor-endowment ratio is somewhere between the $\bar{k}$ axis and curve c. Similarly, we can draw a curve $\bar{c}$ on the $(k\text{-}\bar{k})$ plane so that the *foreign* country is completely specialized in good m *if and only if* the relative factor-endowment ratio is somewhere between the k axis and curve $\bar{c}$. On the basis of this, we separate the $(k\text{-}\bar{k})$ plane into three regions as noted in Figure 3.1.

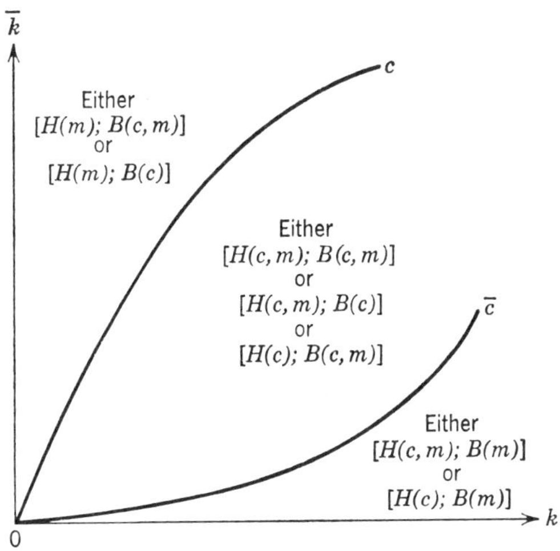

Figure 3.1

In Figure 3.1 in the region between the $\bar{k}$ axis and curve c, the alternative patterns of specialization are $[H(m); B(c, m)]$ or $[H(m); B(c)]$; at some points there may be one pattern, at some points the other, and so on.

Now let us draw the $\dot{k} = 0$ curve on the $(k\text{-}\bar{k})$ plane with the help of (22), (23), (27), (28), and (29). As in Figure 3.2 the $\dot{k} = 0$ curve is composed of a vertical line in the region where the home country is completely specialized in production of capital goods and of a curve of positive slope in the region where the foreign country is completely specialized in capital goods. The $\dot{k} = 0$ curve is downward-sloping for the region where neither of the two countries is completely specialized in capital goods. The $\dot{\bar{k}} = 0$ curve has a

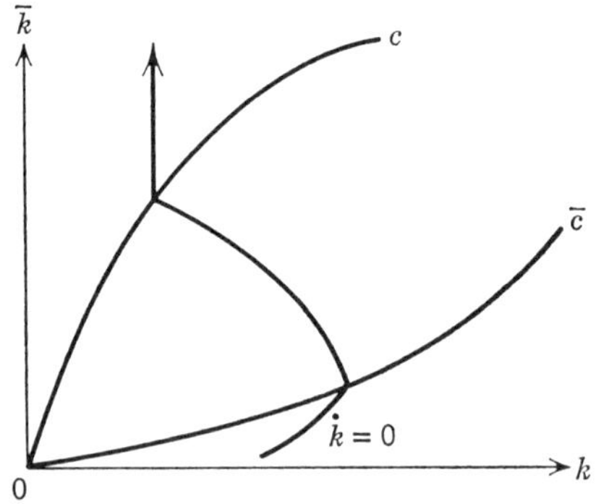

Figure 3.2

similar shape only with the axes inverted. In Figure 3.3 the $\dot{\bar{k}} = 0$ curve is drawn on the (k-$\bar{k}$) plane.

Combining Figures 3.2 and 3.3, we give three illustrations of the dynamic equilibrium positions in Figures 3.4a, 3.4b, and 3.4c. Given the shapes of the $\dot{k} = 0$ and $\dot{\bar{k}} = 0$ curves and given (22) and (27), it is easily seen that there uniquely[9] exists a pair (k^*, $\bar{k}^*$) of capital-labor ratios such that both the countries are in a steady state and $\dot{k} = \dot{\bar{k}} = 0$. The directions of the arrows in Figures 3.4a, 3.4b, and 3.4c clearly indicate global stability of equilibrium, that is, the

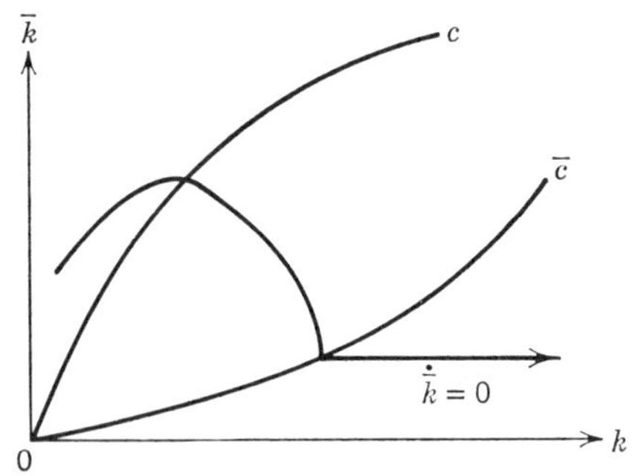

Figure 3.3

[9] For the case of the "classical" savings function, there is a possibility that the $\dot{k} = 0$ and $\dot{\bar{k}} = 0$ curves coincide for a stretch where both the countries are incompletely specialized (as explained in footnote 7), and the equilibrium may not thus be unique.

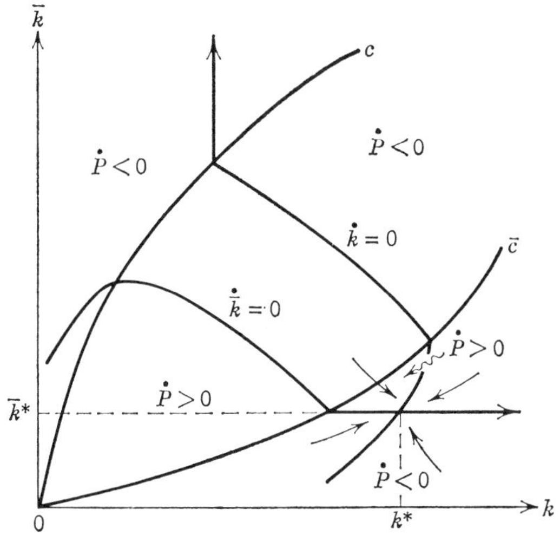

Figure 3.4a

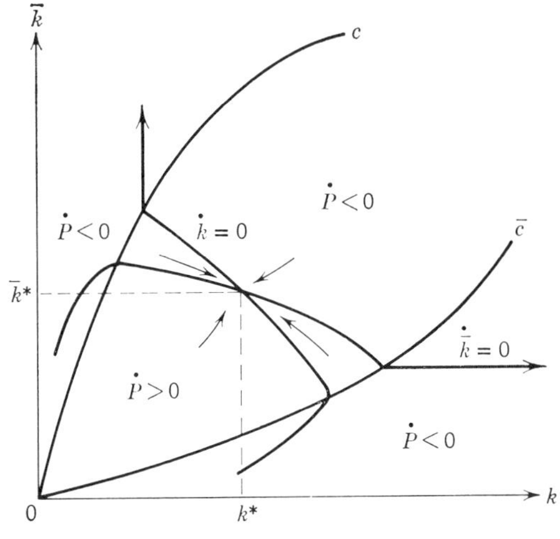

Figure 3.4b

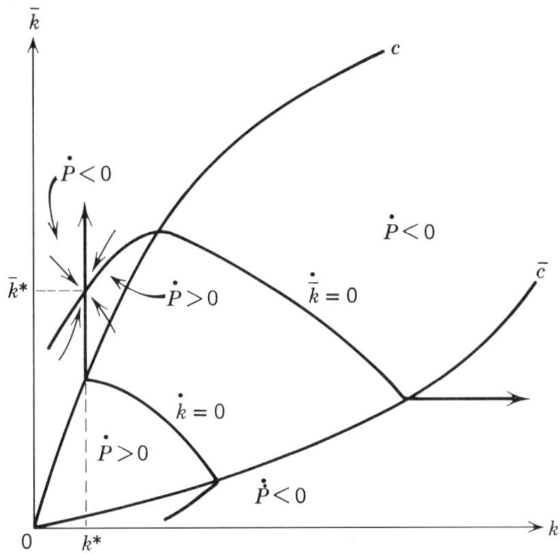

Figure 3.4c

capital-labor ratio of each country eventually converges to the long-run equilibrium value, starting from any initial condition. For proving existence, uniqueness, and stability, the assumption of labor-intensive capital goods seems to be sufficient[10] for the case of proportional savings functions.[11]

This analysis thus describes the time path, starting from an initial condition all the way to the long-run equilibrium position, of the capital-labor ratios of the two trading countries, and since in this model the world price P depends only on these capital-labor ratios, it also describes the time paths of the terms of trade of these two countries. (In contrast, in Chapter 1 we analyzed the impact on terms of trade only of once-and-for-all changes in factor endowments.) In Figures 3.4a, 3.4b, and 3.4c we have indicated the movement of P in some of the regions of the (k-$\bar{k}$) plane; for other regions the nature of movement depends on particular magnitudes in each individual case, but in principle is easily determined because the signs of $\dot{k}$ and $\dot{\bar{k}}$ in each region are known.

[10] For existence and stability of equilibrium in the case of a classical savings function, the extra assumption of $\sigma_c \geq 1$, $\bar{\sigma}_c \geq 1$ are required.

[11] The stability conditions in the case in which capital goods are more capital-intensive seem to be quite complicated (involving elasticities of factor substitution and factor shares in industries) and are not analyzed here.

4

EQUILIBRIUM GROWTH WITH IMPORTED INPUTS

4.1. A NEW MODEL OF TRADE AND GROWTH

In Chapter 3 we extended a simple neoclassical general-equilibrium growth model to the case in which there is balanced trade in consumer and capital goods and analyzed how, from any given initial conditions, the capital-labor ratios in the two economies and the terms of trade approach their long-run equilibrium levels. Although this kind of model provides a fairly general framework for analyzing more complicated issues, it does not focus on (or underplays the role of) some of the important problems emphasized in much of the literature on trade and development. For example, one of the stylized facts of trade and development frequently cited (but less often formally analyzed) in the literature is the supposedly sluggish world demand for exports (particularly of primary commodities) acting as a bottleneck in the growth of a developing economy. In this chapter we develop models in which the home economy faces a world demand for its exports that is price-inelastic and growing at an exogenously determined rate (which may be lower than the domestic growth rate of population, thereby depressing the long-run growth rate of the economy). We analyze the time paths of output, capital stock, imports, and terms of trade in these models and also examine the conditions under which they converge to the long-run equilibrium levels. By introducing the export demand bottleneck, we thus try to contribute toward building a bridge between the neoclassical general-equilibrium models of trade and growth and the underlying models of much of the literature on trade and development.

Second, in Chapter 3 we ignored the possible impact of imports of intermediate products on growth. A very large part of imports of developing countries today consists of intermediate products (such as steel, cement, fertilizers). In Section 4.2 we describe a model in which imports by the home country consist solely of intermediate products not produced at home.

Third, in Section 4.3 we discuss a growth model in which imports consist only of machinery of a type different from that produced at home. We thus try to focus on the important components of the balance of payments of a developing economy and also to go beyond the growth model of Chapter 3 in which the problem of allocating savings among heterogenous capital goods was ignored.

4.2. GROWTH WITH IMPORTS OF INTERMEDIATE PRODUCTS[1]

Since our models involve these extra complications, for obtaining manageable qualitative conclusions we have simplified them somewhat in other respects. For example, throughout this chapter we assume Cobb–Douglas production functions as well as a constant elasticity of export demand with respect to price. Without these assumptions, the analysis would certainly become more complicated, but our basic framework need not be discarded. (We might mention here that Cobb–Douglas production functions, apart from their linear-logarithmic nature, which facilitates all calculations, possess one extra desirable property in the context of our present problem, namely, they make domestic factors *complementary with* imported

[1] A recent independent paper by Khang [56] discusses a model very similar to the one described in this section.

inputs of intermediate products or capital goods in production:[2] this is certainly in line with some of the ideas in development literature.) We also assume throughout that all domestic output (that is consumable, exportable, and investable) is produced on the same production function and that the home economy produces no substitute for the imported inputs. These are obviously simplifying assumptions; a more general model should add to the number of production sectors and analyze all possible patterns of specialization.

In this section we consider intermediate products as the only imported input. The production function for domestic output F is given by

$$F = K^{\alpha} V^{\beta} L^{1-\alpha-\beta}, \tag{1}$$

where K is capital, V is the amount of imported intermediate product, L is labor, and the exponents are given positive constants. Output per unit of labor f is thus given by

$$f = k^{\alpha} v^{\beta}, \tag{2}$$

where k and v are K and V per unit of labor. National income per unit of labor y is given by

$$y = Pf - v, \tag{3}$$

where P is the price of domestic output and the imported good is taken as the *numéraire*. Under free trade P also stands for the terms of trade in this economy. The price of the imported input being equal to the value of its marginal product, we have

$$1 = P \frac{\partial F}{\partial V} = P\beta k^{\alpha} v^{\beta-1}. \tag{4}$$

The balance of trade equation is given by

$$PX = V, \tag{5}$$

where X is the amount of domestic output exported. We assume that the world demand for this export of the home economy is price-inelastic and growing at an exogenously given rate λ, so that

$$X = P^{\eta} e^{\lambda t}, \qquad \text{with} \quad \eta < 0,\ 1 + \eta > 0, \tag{6}$$

[2] In the sense that increased use of imported inputs raises the marginal product of domestic factors of production.

where η is the constant price-elasticity of demand. We assume that labor grows at an exponential rate μ, so that

$$L(t) = L(0)e^{\mu t}. \tag{7}$$

Without any loss of generality, let us put $L(0) = 1$. Now from (4), (5), and (6),

$$v = P^{1+\eta}e^{(\lambda-\mu)t}. \tag{8}$$

As in Chapter 3 we have the simplest savings function whereby a constant fraction s of national income is saved and invested, so that

$$\frac{\dot{K}}{K} = \frac{sy}{Pk}. \tag{9}$$

We are once again ignoring depreciation of capital, but proportional depreciation may be easily introduced. Using (2), (3), and (4), (9) can be rewritten as

$$\frac{\dot{K}}{K} = sk^{\alpha-1}v^{\beta}(1-\beta). \tag{10}$$

Since in the steady state capital should grow at a constant rate, (10) immediately suggests that in the steady state $\underline{k} \equiv k^{1-\alpha}/v^{\beta}$ is a constant. From (4) and (8),

$$\frac{\dot{v}}{v} = \frac{\lambda - \mu - \alpha(1+\eta)\dfrac{\dot{k}}{k}}{1-(1+\eta)(1-\beta)}, \tag{11}$$

where the denominator is positive, since $1 > 1 + \eta > 0$. We are now in a position to write down the basic differential equation of the model:

$$\begin{aligned}\frac{\dot{\underline{k}}}{\underline{k}} &= (1-\alpha)\frac{\dot{k}}{k} - \beta\frac{\dot{v}}{v} = \frac{\dot{k}}{k}\left[(1-\alpha) + \frac{\alpha\beta(1+\eta)}{1-(1-\beta)(1+\eta)}\right] \\ &\quad + \frac{(\mu-\lambda)\beta}{1-(1+\eta)(1-\beta)} \\ &= \frac{\dot{K}}{K}\frac{[\beta - \eta(1-\alpha-\beta)]}{[1-(1-\beta)(1+\eta)]} - \frac{[\lambda\beta - \mu\eta(1-\alpha-\beta)]}{[1-(1-\beta)(1+\eta)]}. \end{aligned} \tag{12}$$

Using (10) in (12),

$$\frac{\dot{\underline{k}}}{\underline{k}} = \frac{s(1-\beta)}{\underline{k}} \frac{[\beta(1+\eta) - \eta(1-\alpha)]}{[1-(1-\beta)(1+\eta)]} - \frac{[\lambda\beta - \mu\eta(1-\alpha-\beta)]}{[1-(1-\beta)(1+\eta)]}, \tag{13}$$

From (12) and (13) we can characterize the time path of this economy in terms of Figure 4.1.

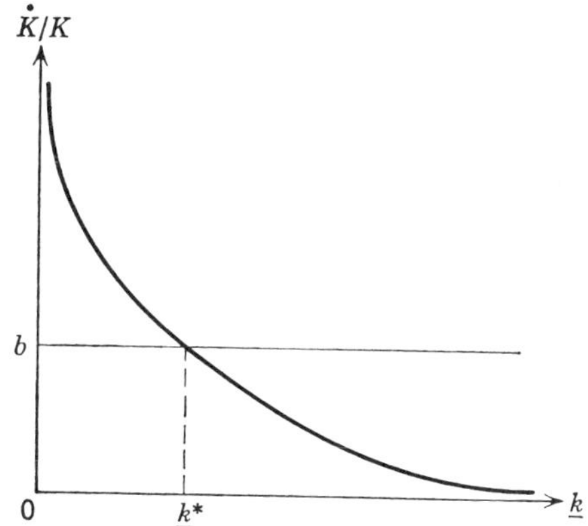

Figure 4.1

In Figure 4.1 the long-run equilibrium rate of growth of capital is

$$b = \frac{\lambda\beta - \mu\eta(1-\alpha-\beta)}{\beta - \eta(1-\alpha-\beta)} > 0,$$

and k^* is the steady-state level of k. Since

$$\frac{\dot{K}}{K} = \frac{s(1-\beta)}{\underline{k}}$$

is a uniformly declining function of $\underline{k}$ and asymptotic to the two axes, the steady state exists, is unique, and is globally stable (that is, from any given initial $\underline{k}$ the economy tends to converge to $\underline{k}^*$).

It is interesting to note that

$$b = \frac{\lambda\beta}{\beta - \eta(1-\alpha-\beta)} - \frac{\mu\eta(1-\alpha-\beta)}{\beta - \eta(1-\alpha-\beta)}$$

is a weighted average of λ and μ.[3] If the exogenous rate of growth in world demand for the home country's exports is smaller than its rate of growth of population (which is observed in a number of developing countries today, India being a major example), the long-run equilibrium rate of growth of capital is *lower* than its "natural" rate of growth (in this case, the rate of growth of population). In other words, if $\mu > \lambda$, $b < \mu$.[4] This in some sense highlights the depressing impact of a sluggish world demand for exports on the long-run equilibrium rate of growth of an economy. In the usual neo-classical growth model, the long-run growth rate of the economy is equal to the natural rate of growth unaffected by demand conditions. In our model, however, the long-run growth rate is influenced by conditions of world demand for exports because the latter affect the rate of growth of availability of imported inputs used in domestic production.

It might also be noted that $db/d\lambda > 0$, that is, the smaller the exogenous growth rate of world demand, the smaller the long-run growth rate, and that for $\lambda < \mu$, $db/d\eta < 0$, that is, the smaller the *absolute value* of the price elasticity of demand for exports, the

[3] In a neoclassical growth model with Cobb–Douglas production functions, if two factors grow at given rates (L growing at the given rate of population growth and the growth rate of V being determined by the rate of growth of export demand), it is not surprising to find the steady-state rate of growth of capital to be equal to a weighted average of these two rates. If the production functions were not Cobb–Douglas, the weights would change as the economy moves toward the steady state. When the elasticity of factor substitution is greater than unity, the weights tend to shift increasingly toward the faster-growing factor, while if the elasticity of substitution is less than unity the rate of growth of the slower growing factor determines the steady-state rate.

[4] It should be pointed out that b is the long-run equilibrium rate of growth of capital and not that of national income. The latter is $\dot{Y}/Y = \dot{P}/P + \dot{K}/K$ in the steady state (since in the steady state $\dot{K}/K$ and therefore the right-hand side of (9) is constant). Since from (14) $\dot{P}/P < 0$ in the steady state for $\mu > \lambda$, $\dot{Y}/Y < b$. In other words, the long-run equilibrium rate of growth of national income is less than that of capital, and *a fortiori* less than the rate of growth of population. So, in this model in the steady-state per capita income is declining. Certainly this kind of a situation cannot go on forever in the real world; besides, there are off-setting factors such as technical progress, foreign aid, and so on. The major purpose of this chapter is only to focus on the demand limitation on growth.

It may also be easily confirmed that the equilibrium rate of growth of national income is smaller, the smaller the exogenous rate of growth of world demand and/or the smaller the absolute value of price elasticity of demand for exports.

smaller the long-run rate of growth. Both of these results are quite plausible.

What happens to terms of trade over time? From (4) and (11),

$$[1-(1+\eta)(1-\beta)]\frac{\dot{P}}{P}=\alpha\mu-(\mu-\lambda)(1-\beta)-\alpha\frac{\dot{K}}{K}. \qquad (14)$$

For $\underline{k} \leq \underline{k}^*$, $\dot{K}/K \geq b$, and it is easy to see from (14) that $\dot{P}/P < 0$ if $\mu > \lambda$; so terms of trade for the home country *decline* over time for $\underline{k}$ not exceeding its steady-state level. Imports as a proportion of national income, however, remain constant over time, since

$$\frac{V}{Y}=\frac{1}{\dfrac{PF}{V}-1}=\frac{\beta}{1-\beta}.$$

The so-called "golden rule" for maximum steady-state level of per capita consumption in this model appears somewhat different from the usual condition of marginal product of capital equalized to the rate of growth, but this can be easily interpreted. Per capita consumption in this economy is given by

$$c=\frac{y}{P}-\frac{\dot{K}}{L}. \qquad (15)$$

Since in the steady state $\dot{K}/K = b$, (15) may be rewritten as

$$c=\frac{y}{P}-bk. \qquad (16)$$

The "golden rule" is therefore given by the following condition:

$$\frac{d\left(\dfrac{y}{P}\right)}{dk}=b. \qquad (17)$$

Since y/P is per capita real income in this model, (17) means that the "golden rule" is to equalize the marginal contribution of capital (direct as well as indirect through its impact on the amount of imported input used) to real income with the rate of growth of capital. Since from (2) and (3), $y/P = (1-\beta)k^{\alpha}v^{\beta}$, (17) implies that

$$(1-\beta)k^{\alpha-1}v^{\beta}\left[\alpha+\beta\frac{dv}{dk}\frac{k}{v}\right]=b. \qquad (18)$$

From (4) and (8), for a given t,

$$\frac{dv}{dk}\frac{k}{v} = \frac{-\alpha(1+\eta)}{1-(1+\eta)(1-\beta)}. \tag{19}$$

Using (19), (18) may be rewritten as

$$\frac{\alpha k^{\alpha-1}v^{\beta}(1-\beta)(-\eta)}{1-(1+\eta)(1-\beta)} = b. \tag{20}$$

From (20) it is easy to see that the "golden rule" in this model implies that the rate of growth of capital b should be *smaller* than $k^{\alpha-1}v^{\beta}$, which is the direct marginal product of capital in the production functions.

Before ending this section we might note that in (6) it has been assumed that the world demand for the export of the home economy is price-inelastic (that is, $1 + \eta > 0$), but nowhere in the calculations in this section has this been used. Although this assumption will play an important role in the next section, all the qualitative conclusions made so far are valid even if export demand is price-elastic (or $1 + \eta \leq 0$). These conclusions are, however, sensitive to the assumption that world demand grows at an exogenous rate lower than the rate of population growth. We might briefly indicate here how these conclusions will change if we relax this assumption (after all, there are some underdeveloped countries—at least the oil-exporting ones—for which λ may be well above μ). The proof of existence, uniqueness, and global stability of long-run equilibrium is, of course, unaltered. The equilibrium growth rate of capital b, however, is now larger than (equal to) μ, since λ is larger than (equal to) μ. Besides, $db/d\lambda$ is still positive, but $db/d\lambda \geq 0$ for $\lambda \geq \mu$. In the steady state, terms of trade improve (remain constant) for λ larger than (equal to) μ. The steady-state per capita income is also increasing for $\lambda > \mu$, and the "golden rule" discussion remains unaltered.

4.3. GROWTH WITH TWO TYPES OF CAPITAL

In this section we analyze another model which is similar to the preceding one in many respects, but now imports consist only of foreign machines which are different from domestically produced machines. The production function for domestic output F is given by

$$F = K_1^{\alpha} K_2^{\beta} L^{1-\alpha-\beta} \tag{21}$$

where K_1 is domestic capital and K_2 is foreign capital, all of which is imported. Output per capita f is thus

$$f = k_1^{\alpha} k_2^{\beta}. \tag{22}$$

The rental rates, $R_i (i = 1, 2)$, on capital are given by the marginal value productivity conditions, or

$$R_1 = P \frac{\partial f}{\partial k_1} = P\alpha k_1^{\alpha-1} k_2^{\beta} \tag{23}$$

$$R_2 = P \frac{\partial f}{\partial k_2} = P\beta k_1^{\alpha} k_2^{\beta-1}, \tag{24}$$

where P, as before, is the price of domestic output (under free trade, also the terms of trade) with the imported good taken as the *numéraire*. The balance of trade equation is given by

$$PX = \dot{K}_2. \tag{25}$$

Physical depreciation of both types of capital will be ignored. As before, labor grows at an exponential rate μ, with $L(0) = 1$, and a constant proportion s of the national income is saved and invested so that

$$sPF = P\dot{K}_1 + \dot{K}_2. \tag{26}$$

We have yet to introduce an equation that determines the demand for either type of capital (that is, allocation of investment between the two capital goods). Suppose demand for capital stock of either type depends only on the value of total wealth and the two own rates of return on capital. More specifically, we assume the following demand function for K_2:[5]

$$K_2 = Jg\left(\frac{R_1}{P}, R_2\right), \tag{27}$$

[5] The justification of the stock demand function (27) is based on considerations of portfolio diversification discussed by Tobin [91]. These are in terms of risk-avoiding strategy where one or both yields are imperfectly predictable. A similar

where $J = PK_1 + K_2$ is the total value of wealth and the wealth elasticity of demand for K_2 is assumed to be unity (for simplification). It is plausible to suppose (under the assumption that the probability distributions for the two rates of return are independent and are not affected by changes in K_1 and K_2) that demand for K_2 varies positively with changes in its own rate of return R_2, so that $g_2 = \partial g/\partial R_2 > 0$, and that it varies inversely with changes in the own rate of return on the other capital, so that

$$g_1 = \frac{\partial g}{\partial\left(\frac{R_1}{P}\right)} < 0.$$

As in the preceding section, it is assumed that the world demand for exports of the home economy is price-inelastic and growing at an exogenously given rate. Let us for the time being also assume that this given rate of growth of demand happens to be equal to the home country's rate of population growth (that is, $\mu = \lambda$). We shall refer

---

demand function, with money and capital as assets, is used in a growth model by Tobin [92], p. 679.

In the riskless case the condition for allocation between the two assets will be $R_1/P = R_2$. With our assumption of Cobb–Douglas production function, both types of capital goods are essential for production, and efficient allocation under these circumstances will lead to the interior solution where the rates of return are equalized. From (23) and (24) this immediately gives us

$$P = \frac{\alpha}{\beta}\frac{k_2}{k_1}$$

This means that the terms of trade are a declining (increasing) function of k_1 (k_2). It is easy to check that the steady state in this model is unique and stable (with the phase diagram exactly as in Figure 4.2) under the sufficient condition that the absolute value of the price elasticity of demand for export is large enough (more precisely, $\alpha + \eta < 0$).

All this, however, assumes that one can freely switch from one asset to another. It may sometimes be better to assume a flow demand function rather than a stock demand function such that

$$\frac{\dot{K}_2}{sPF}\begin{cases} = 0 \\ \varepsilon[0, 1] \\ = 1 \end{cases} \quad \text{as} \quad \frac{R_1}{P} \gtreqless R_2$$

The case is worked out in details in the Appendix to this chapter.

to the more interesting cases of $\mu \neq \lambda$ at the end of this section. Thus, we have

$$X = P^{\eta} e^{\mu t}, \qquad \text{with } \eta < 0 \qquad \text{and} \qquad 1 + \eta > 0. \tag{28}$$

Using (23) and (24), let us rewrite (27) in per capita terms as

$$[Pk_1 + k_2] g(\alpha k_1^{\alpha-1} k_2^{\beta}, P\beta k_1^{\alpha} k_2^{\beta-1}) - k_2 = 0. \tag{29}$$

This gives P, the terms of trade, as a function of k_1 and k_2. From (29), the elasticity of P with respect to k_1, or

$$\frac{\partial P}{\partial k_1}\frac{k_1}{P} = E_{p1} = -\frac{[(1-g) + e_1(1-\alpha) + e_2\alpha]}{(1 - g + e_2)} < 0, \tag{30}$$

where $e_2 = (g_2 R_2)/g$ is the elasticity of the g function (the function that gives the proportion of total wealth kept in terms of imported capital K_2) with respect to its own rate of return R_2; and $e_1 = -(g_1 R_1)/Pg$ is the (positively defined) elasticity of the g function with respect to the own rate of return on the other type of capital K_1. Since from (29) $1 > g > 0$ (with positive amounts of both capital), E_{p1} is negative. This means that terms of trade for the home country decline with accumulation per capita of domestic capital. From (29) again, the elasticity of P with respect to k_2, or

$$\frac{\partial P}{\partial k_2}\frac{k_2}{P} = E_{p2} = \frac{[(1-g) + e_1\beta + e_2(1-\beta)]}{(1-g) + e_2} > 0. \tag{31}$$

This means that terms of trade *improve* with accumulation per capita of foreign capital. Since $E_{p1} + E_{p2} \geq 0$ for $e_2 - e_1 \geq 0$, the terms of trade will improve under this condition if k_2 grows at a higher rate than k_1.

We may now write down the two differential equations in the system. From (25), (28), and (29), and letting $L(0) = 1$, the rate of accumulation of k_2 is given by (32).

$$\frac{\dot{k}_2}{k_2} = \frac{P^{1+\eta}}{k_2} - \mu = \Phi(k_1, k_2). \tag{32}$$

From (22), (26), and (32), the rate of accumulation of k_1 is given by (33):

$$\frac{\dot{k}_1}{k_1} = sk_1^{\alpha-1}k_2^{\beta} - \frac{P^{\eta}}{k_1} - \mu = \Psi(k_1, k_2). \tag{33}$$

Let us now analyze the properties of these two differential equations. Since $E_{p1} < 0$ from (30), and $1 + \eta > 0$ in (32),

$$\Phi_1 = \frac{\partial \Phi}{\partial k_1} < 0. \tag{34}$$

Since from (31), $E_{p2} \leq 1$ for $e_2 \geq e_1$, $(1 + \eta)E_{p2} < 1$ and, therefore in (32)

$$\Phi_2 = \frac{\partial \Phi}{\partial k_2} < 0. \tag{35}$$

Thus, under the sufficient condition $e_2 \geq e_1$, that is, the own elasticity in the g function is larger than or equal to the cross-elasticity,

$$\left(\frac{dk_1}{dk_2}\right)_{\Phi=0} = -\frac{\Phi_2}{\Phi_1} < 0, \tag{36}$$

so that the $\dot{k}_2 = 0$ curve is downward-sloping in the (k_1, k_2) plane, as shown in Figure 4.2. From (33),

$$\Psi_1 = \frac{\partial \Psi}{\partial k_1} = \frac{1}{k_1^2}\left[-(1-\alpha)sk_1^{\alpha}k_2^{\beta} + P^{\eta}(1 - \eta E_{p1})\right]. \tag{37}$$

Since from (33) it follows that along $\Psi = 0$, $sk_1^{\alpha}k_2^{\beta} > P^{\eta}$,

$$(\Psi_1)_{\Psi=0} < 0 \tag{38}$$

if $\eta E_{p1} \geq \alpha$; from (30) it is easy to see that a (strongly) sufficient condition for the latter is that the absolute value of the price elasticity of demand for exports is large enough, that is,

$$|\eta| \geq \frac{\alpha e_2}{\alpha e_2 + (1-\alpha)e_1}. \tag{39}$$

Since from (31) $E_{p2} > 0$, it immediately follows from (33) that

$$\Psi_2 = \frac{\partial \Psi}{\partial k_2} > 0. \tag{40}$$

Thus, under the sufficient condition of (39),

$$\left(\frac{dk_1}{dk_2}\right)_{\Psi=0} = -\left(\frac{\Psi_2}{\Psi_1}\right)_{\Psi=0} > 0, \tag{41}$$

so that the $\dot{k}_1 = 0$ curve is upward-sloping in the $(k_1\text{-}k_2)$ plane, as shown in Figure 4.2.

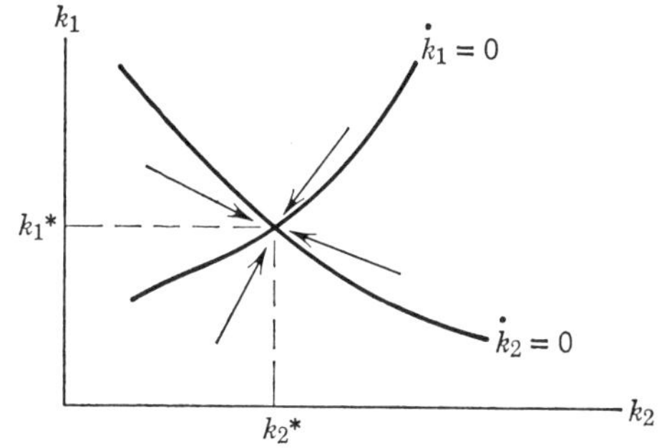

Figure 4.2

From Figure 4.2 the steady state in this model is unique and stable,[6] that is, starting from any initial k_1 and k_2 the system tends to converge to a unique set of k_1^* and k_2^*. The (strongly) sufficient conditions for this are, along with the general assumptions of the model, (a) the own elasticity in the asset allocation function g is not smaller than the cross-elasticity and (b) the price elasticity of demand for exports is large enough (though less than unity). The arrows in Figure 4.2 indicate the possible time paths of k_1 and k_2, and therefore P, the terms of trade.

Let us now refer to the case in which $\mu \neq \lambda$, in particular when the world demand for exports is growing at a sufficiently sluggish rate so that $\mu > \lambda$. The only change involved will be in (28), so that now $X = P^{\eta} e^{\lambda t}$. The analysis of the differential equations of the system now becomes more complicated. We can briefly report the results around the steady state, however. In the steady state the rate of growth of capital of each type is constant, so that

$$\frac{\dot{K}_2}{K_2} \left(= \frac{P^{1+\eta}}{K_2} e^{\lambda t} \right)$$

is a constant and

$$\frac{\dot{K}_1}{K_1} \left(= s k_1^{\alpha - 1} k_2^{\beta} - \frac{\dot{K}_2}{P K_1} \right)$$

is also a constant. Since from (29) P is still only a function of k_1 and

[6] Since Φ_2 and Ψ_1 are negative, the trace of the Jacobian matrix evaluated around equilibrium in the two differential equations (32) and (33) is negative and hence by the Bendixson Theorem limit cycles are ruled out.

k_2, with the use of (30) and (31) we can work out the steady-state rates of growth. They are as follows:

$$\frac{\dot{K}_1}{K_1} = \frac{\mu(1-\alpha-\beta)(1-\eta)+\lambda\beta}{(1-\alpha)-\eta(1-\alpha-\beta)} \tag{42}$$

$$\frac{\dot{K}_2}{K_2} = \frac{\lambda(1-\alpha)-\eta\mu(1-\alpha-\beta)}{(1-\alpha)-\eta(1-\alpha-\beta)}. \tag{43}$$

Both of these rates of growth of capital are weighted averages of μ and λ, so that in the steady state k_1 and k_2 decline, remain constant, or increase as μ is greater than, equal to, or less than λ. The rate of growth of national income is the same as that of K_1. Both of these rates of growth are increasing (decreasing) functions of the absolute value of the price elasticity of demand for exports if μ is larger (smaller) than λ. An increase in λ, the rate of growth of world demand, however, always increases the rates of growth. It also turns out that in the steady state

$$\frac{\dot{P}}{P} = \frac{\dot{K}_2}{K_2} - \frac{\dot{K}_1}{K_1} = \frac{(\lambda-\mu)(1-\alpha-\beta)}{(1-\alpha)-\eta(1-\alpha-\beta)}. \tag{44}$$

This means that in the steady state terms of trade are *declining* (improving) if the world demand is sluggish (buoyant) enough so that μ is larger (smaller) than λ.

We also carried out the *local* stability analysis for the steady state in this model. The differential equations in the system (involving the rate of growth of the rates of growth of each type of capital) are locally stable if the elasticities in the asset allocation function g are constant and if the own elasticity e_2 is not smaller than the cross-elasticity e_1. Figure 4.3 shows some of the relevant properties of this system.

In summary, in this chapter we have analyzed, in the framework of two simple dynamic models, the limitation imposed on growth by the nature of world demand for a country's exports when imports consist of intermediate products or capital goods that are not produced at home. The time paths of output, capital stocks, imports, and terms of trade have been analyzed in terms of the properties of the fundamental differential equations of the system.

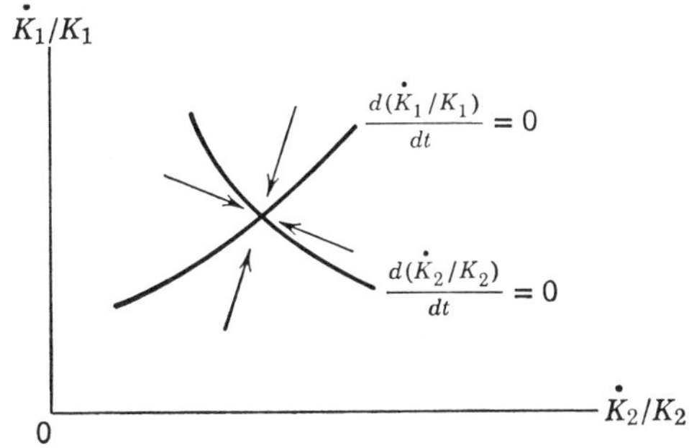

Figure 4.3

APPENDIX

Here we replace (27) by a flow demand function so that

$$\frac{\dot{K}_2}{sPF}\begin{cases} = 0 \\ \varepsilon[0, 1] \\ = 1 \end{cases} \quad \text{as} \quad \frac{R_1}{P} \gtreqless R_2 \tag{45}$$

Let us first take the interior case when $R_1/P = R_2$. From (23) and (24) this means that

$$P = \frac{\alpha}{\beta}\frac{k_1}{k_2} \tag{46}$$

with (46) giving P as a function of k_1 and k_2, we may rewrite differential equations (32) and (33) as

$$\frac{\dot{k}_2}{k_2} = \left(\frac{\alpha}{\beta}\right)^{1+\eta} k_2{}^{\eta} k_1^{-(1+\eta)} - \mu = \Phi(k_1, k_2) \tag{47}$$

$$\frac{\dot{k}_1}{k_1} = \left[sk_1^{\alpha-1}k_2{}^{\beta} - \left(\frac{\alpha}{\beta}\right)^{\eta} k_2{}^{\eta} k_1^{-(1+\eta)}\right] - \mu = \Psi(k_1, k_2) \tag{48}$$

It is easy to check that if $\alpha + \eta < 0$ and with $1 + \eta > 0$, $\Phi_1 < 0$, $\Phi_2 < 0$, $\Psi_1 < 0$, $\Psi_2 > 0$, so that the phase diagram for this interior case is exactly as in Figure 4.2.

In the case when $\dot{K}_2 = sPF$ or $\dot{K}_1 = 0$, one can check from (22), (25), (26), and (28) that

$$P = [sk_1{}^{\alpha}k_2{}^{\beta}]^{1/\eta}. \tag{49}$$

From (23), (24), and (49) we can write for this specialization region:

$$R_2 - \frac{R_1}{P} = k_1^{\alpha-1} k_2^{\beta-1} [\beta s^{1/\eta} k_1^{(\alpha+\eta)/\eta} k_2^{\beta/\eta} - \alpha k_2] \tag{50}$$

In Figure 4.4 curve B represents the combination of k_1 and k_2 for

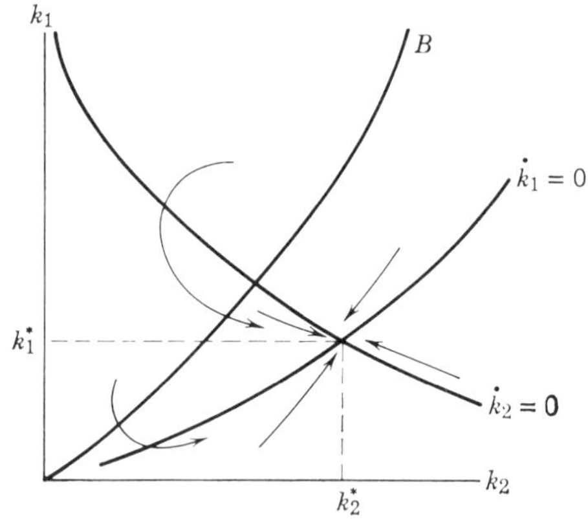

Figure 4.4

which the right-hand side of (50) is just equal to zero. In other words, B represents the boundary between the interior and the specialization region where $\dot{K}_1 = 0$. The latter specialization region lies between curve B and the vertical axis. In this region

$$\dot{k}_2 = s^{(1+\eta)/\eta} k_1^{[\alpha(1+\eta)]/\eta} k_2^{[\beta(1+\eta)]/\eta} - \mu k_2 \tag{51}$$

$$\dot{k}_1 = -\mu k_1 \tag{52}$$

The movements of k_1 and k_2 are accordingly indicated in Figure 4.4. It is easy to prove that the other specialization region where $\dot{K}_2 = 0$ (and consequently $P = 0$) is empty. Thus Figure 4.4 summarizes the time paths of k_1 and k_2 for all feasible cases. The long-run equilibrium (k_1^*, k_2^*) is unique and globally stable. The arrows indicate the possible time paths of k_1 and k_2, hence of the terms of trade.

5

EMBODIED TECHNICAL PROGRESS, ECONOMIC LIFE OF MACHINES, AND COMPARATIVE ADVANTAGE

5.1. THE TWO-SECTOR "CLAY-CLAY" MODEL

In Chapter 1 we discussed the impact of technical progress and international differences in production functions on comparative advantage. There is, however, one important aspect of technical progress that is hardly discussed in the literature on trade theory. If we have a so-called vintage-capital model in which machines unalterably embody the technology of their date of construction, technical progress and the consequent rise in wages reduce the quasi rents on any given old machine and make some old machines *economically* obsolete, that is, unprofitable to operate at current wages. Different countries with different wage rates will therefore have different economic lives of machines even if "best-practice" technology (or technology on the newest machine) is the same everywhere. Since *average* productivity in any industry significantly depends on how modern or outdated its capital stock is, intercountry distribution of comparative advantage depends on intercountry variations in economic lives of capital. To give an example, let us quote Salter [82], pp. 72–73.

"In fact, there is some evidence to suggest that one of the chief reasons for Anglo-American productivity differences lies in standards of obsolescence. It is a common theme in Productivity Mission Reports that the productivity of the best plants in the United Kingdom is comparable with that of the best plants in the United States, and that the difference lies in a much higher proportion of plants employing outmoded methods in the United Kingdom—a much greater 'tail' of low-productivity plants. Such a situation is consistent with a higher standard of obsolescence in the United States which follows from a higher level of real wages."

As we have noted before, the theory of comparative advantage is essentially concerned with the factors determining pretrade equilibrium relative prices, and a comparison of two equiliurium positions for the same (closed) economy with some intervening changes in parameters is a useful way of analyzing those factors. In this chapter also we compare two equilibrium positions of the same economy, when one equilibrium is characterized by a higher wage rate or a lower interest rate and, consequently, a different economic life of capital, with all the other parameters (including the rate of technical progress embodied in new machines) remaining the same, and we are interested in finding the difference in relative commodity prices. This will give us some idea about the impact of differences in economic life of capital on comparative costs. Since the properties of a vintage-capital model off the steady state are very difficult to analyze, we confine ourselves to a comparison of *long-run* equilibria; in other words, our way of analyzing comparative advantage is an exercise in what is known as comparative dynamics.

In the model in this chapter we obviously depart from the assumption of perfect malleability of capital that characterizes virtually all of standard international trade theory. Technical progress is embodied only in new machines, and it continually differentiates new machines from old. Associated with machines produced at any particular point in time, there exists a distinct production function. For simplification we shall take the extreme case[1] in which there is

[1] An important extension of the model in this chapter will be to consider the case in which there is substitution between capital *ex ante* but not *ex post*. This

no scope for substitution between labor and capital at all, either *ex ante* (that is, when it is being decided what kind of machine should be built) or *ex post* (that is, when the machine has been built). In common parlance among economists this is now known as the "clay-clay" model, similar to the one introduced by Solow et al. [90]. Physical depreciation is ignored (again for simplification and for concentrating on the variations in *economic* life of capital), and obsolescence takes its toll when rising wages absorb all the revenues from a particular machine.

There are two sectors in the economy, a consumer goods sector (denoted by c) and a capital goods sector (denoted by m). We have fixed-coefficients production functions for machines of each vintage in each sector:

$$F_i(v, t) = \min\{a_i(v)I_i(v), b_i(v)L_i(v, t)\}, \qquad i = c, m, \tag{1}$$

where $F_i(v, t)\,dv$ and $L_i(v, t)\,dv$ are the rates of output produced and labor employed, respectively, at time t on machines of vintage v [that is, capital installed during a period $(v, v + dv)$ with $v \leq t$] in the ith sector; $a_i(v)$ and $b_i(v)$ are the output per machine and output per man, respectively, using machines of vintage v; $I_i(v)$ is the number of machines of vintage v in the ith sector. In the long-run equilibrium, with no excess of capital or labor, (1) can be written as:

$$F_i(v, t) = a_i(v)I_i(v) = b_i(v)L_i(v, t), \qquad i = c, m. \tag{2}$$

The total output in the ith sector is

$$F_i(t) = \int_{t-T_i}^{t} F_i(v, t)\,dv, \qquad i = c, m, \tag{3}$$

where T_i is the age of the oldest machine in use. In the long-run equilibrium T_i is independent of t.

The total labor supply is divided between the two sectors:

$$L(t) = \int_{t-T_m}^{t} L_m(v, t)\,dv + \int_{t-T_c}^{t} L_c(v, t)\,dv. \tag{4}$$

case is much more difficult to analyze. Besides, for a meaningful comparative-dynamic exercise, the relevant long-run equilibrium should be unique and stable. Whereas, Solow et al. [90] have proved the stability properties of the "clay-clay" model, no one has yet made a similar analysis of the general "putty-clay" model with perfect foresight. For an attempt to prove uniqueness and local stability in the general "putty-clay" model, see Bardhan [14].

A consumer good at each time t is used as a *numéraire*, and $P(t)$ is the price per unit of new capital goods at time t. Pure competition prevails. A machine is scrapped[2] when the wage costs for operating it exhaust the value of its output, so that

$$W(t) = b_c(t - T_c) = P(t)b_m(t - T_m), \tag{5}$$

where $W(t)$ is the wage rate at time t in terms of consumer goods.

Technical progress in this model consists of improvement in the output-input coefficients. Let us assume that technical progress is Harrod-neutral (that is, purely labor-augmenting) at a constant rate g which is uniform in the two sectors. Entrepreneurs (correctly) expect the wage rate to grow at rate g, which is the rate of growth of labor productivity on new machines in either sector. Thus,

$$b_i(t) = b_i e^{gt} \tag{6}$$

and

$$a_i(t) = a_i, \tag{7}$$

where a_i and b_i are given constants; $i = c, m$.

As technical progress is Harrod-neutral and uniform in the two sectors, P is constant in the steady state, so that $P(t) = P$.

The quasi rent (in terms of the *numéraire*) $R_i(v, t)\, dv$ in the ith sector earned at time t per machine of vintage v is:

$$R_c(v, t) = a_c\left[1 - \frac{W(t)}{b_c(v)}\right] \tag{8}$$

and

$$R_m(v, t) = Pa_m\left[1 - \frac{W(t)}{Pb_m(v)}\right] \tag{9}$$

With equilibrium in the capital market, the present value of quasi

[2] We are, of course, assuming that there is no resale value for old machines. This ignores, among other things, the significant phenomenon of trade in second-hand machinery. If there is a backward economy with lower wages that is prepared to buy machines rendered economically obsolete by the higher wages in the advanced country, this might introduce an extra dimension to the model and through the marginal scrapping condition some link between the variables in the two countries can be analyzed. We have not attempted this analysis here. For a note on international trade in second-hand equipment, see Sen [87].

rents of a new machine over its economic lifetime should be equal to its cost of production. Thus, if r is the rate of interest and if it is expected to remain constant,[3] for the capital goods sector,

$$P = \int_{v}^{v+T_m} T_m(v, t)e^{-r(t-v)}\,dt$$

$$= a_m P \int_{v}^{v+T_m} e^{-r(t-v)}[1 - e^{g(t-v-T_m)}]\,dt. \tag{10}$$

Using (5), (6), and (9) in (10) and integrating,[3] we obtain

$$1 = a_m\left[\frac{1 - e^{-rT_m}}{r} + \frac{e^{-rT_m} - e^{-gT_m}}{r-g}\right]. \tag{11}$$

Similarly, for the consumer goods sector,

$$P = \int_{v}^{v+T_c} R_c(v, t)e^{-r(t-v)}\,dt = a_c \int_{v}^{v+T_c} e^{-r(t-v)}[1 - e^{g(t-v-T_c)}], \tag{12}$$

or using (5), (6), and (8), and integrating,[4]

$$P = a_c\left[\frac{1 - e^{-rT_c}}{r} + \frac{e^{-rT_c} - e^{-gT_c}}{r-g}\right]. \tag{13}$$

5.2. COMPARATIVE ADVANTAGE

In Section 5.1 we described some of the characteristics of a long-run equilibrium in a two-sector model of embodied technical progress

[3] Solow et al. [90], pp. 101–102, have proved that with exponential, purely labor-augmenting, technical progress in the "clay-clay" model, the only competitive equilibrium interest rate compatible with balanced growth is a constant interest rate.

[4] In (11) and (13) it is assumed that $r \neq g$. If $r = g$, (11) must be rewritten as

$$1 = a_m\left[\frac{1 - e^{-rT_m}}{r} - T_m e^{-rT_m}\right] \tag{11a}$$

and (13) must be rewritten as

$$P = a_c\left[\frac{1 - e^{-rT_c}}{r} - T_c e^{-rT_c}\right]. \tag{11b}$$

with economic obsolescence of machines. In this section we carry out a comparative-dynamic exercise of comparing two long-run equilibria with different r, the rate of interest,[5] and find out what it implies in terms of difference in P, the price ratio, that is, the comparative cost ratio in a two-country model. In other words, we are interested in the sign of dP/dr, comparing two long-run equilibria.

From (5) and (6),

$$P = \frac{b_c(t - T_c)}{b_m(t - T_m)} = \frac{b_c}{b_m} e^{g(T_m - T_c)}. \tag{14}$$

From (14),

$$\operatorname{sign} \frac{dP}{dr} = \operatorname{sign}\left[\frac{dT_m}{dr} - \frac{dT_c}{dr}\right] = \operatorname{sign} \frac{dT_m}{dr}\left[1 - \frac{dT_c}{dT_m}\right]. \tag{15}$$

Let us now define the right-hand side of (11) as $a_m \phi(r, T_m)$ for a given g, and the right-hand side of equation (13) as $a_c \phi(r, T_c)$. From (11),

$$\frac{dT_m}{dr} = -\frac{\phi_r(r, T_m)}{\phi_{T_m}(r, T_m)}, \tag{16}$$

where

$$\phi_r = \frac{\partial \phi(r, T_m)}{\partial r} \qquad \text{and} \qquad \phi_{T_m} = \frac{\partial \phi(r, T_m)}{\partial T_m}.$$

From (10) and (12) it can be shown directly (putting $v = 0$) that

$$\phi_r(r, T_i) = \int_0^{T_i} (-t)e^{-rt}[1 - e^{g(t - T_i)}]\, dt < 0, \qquad i = c, m \tag{17}$$

Equations (11) and (13) may be rewritten, so that

$$\phi(r, T_i) = \frac{1}{r}\left[1 + \frac{(ge^{-rT_i} - re^{-gT_i})}{r - g}\right], \qquad i = c, m. \tag{18}$$

From (18),

$$\phi_{T_i}(r, T_i) > 0, \qquad i = c, m. \tag{19}$$

[5] In long-run equilibria of this model a higher interest rate implies a lower wage rate. From (5) and (6), $W(t) = b_c e^{g(t - T_c)}$ and since our subsequent analysis shows $dT_c/dr > 0$, $dW/dr < 0$.

From (16), (17), and (19),

$$\frac{dT_m}{dr} > 0. \tag{20}$$

This means that the long-run equilibrium with a higher rate of interest will have a *longer* economic life of capital in the capital goods sector.

Now from (13) and (14),

$$a_c \phi(r, T_c) - \frac{b_c}{b_m} e^{g(T_m - T_c)} = 0. \tag{21}$$

Since T_m is a function of r, (21) gives us the following implicit function:

$$G(T_m, T_c) = 0. \tag{22}$$

From (22),

$$\left[1 - \frac{dT_c}{dT_m}\right] = 1 + \frac{G_1}{G_2}, \tag{23}$$

where $G_1 = \partial G/\partial T_m$ and $G_2 = \partial G/\partial T_c$.
From (21) and (22),

$$G_1 = \frac{a_c \phi_r(r, T_c)}{\dfrac{dT_m}{dr}} - g \frac{b_c}{b_m} e^{g(T_m - T_c)} \tag{24}$$

and

$$G_2 = a_c \phi_{T_c}(r, T_c) + g \frac{b_c}{b_m} e^{g(T_m - T_c)}. \tag{25}$$

Using (17), (19), and (20) in (24) and (25),

$$G_1 < 0, \qquad G_2 > 0. \tag{26}$$

So from (15), (20), (23), and (26),

$$\text{sign} \frac{dP}{dr} = \text{sign}\,[G_1 + G_2]. \tag{27}$$

In the Appendix to this chapter (27) is shown to be positive or negative as T_m is larger or smaller than T_c.

Now which sector has the longer economic life of capital? From (11), (13), and (14),[6]

$$\frac{a_m b_c}{a_c b_m} = \frac{(r-g)e^{gT_c} + ge^{-(r-g)T_c} - r}{(r-g)e^{gT_m} + ge^{-(r-g)T_m} - r} = \frac{H(T_c)}{H(T_m)} \tag{28}$$

Since it is easy to confirm that

$$\frac{H(T_c)}{H(T_m)} \lesseqgtr 1 \quad \text{as} \quad T_m \gtreqless T_c, \tag{29}$$

we can say that

$$T_m \gtreqless T_c \quad \text{as} \quad \frac{a_c}{b_c} \gtreqless \frac{a_m}{b_m}, \tag{30}$$

or as the capital goods sector is more or less capital-intensive than the consumer goods sector. The more capital-intensive sector has the longer economic life of capital.

Thus, we have proved that $dP/dr \gtreqless 0$ as the capital goods sector is more or less capital-intensive than the consumer goods sector. Between two long-run equilibria, if the rate of interest differs (and therefore the wage rate and the economic life of capital T_i in each sector), the equilibrium with the lower r will have a lower price for the output of the sector in which the capital-labor ratio employed is higher. Let us define the country with the lower interest rate (and higher wage rate) as the more capital-rich country. Then, analyzing across the two countries in long-run equilibria otherwise identical, this means that the more capital-rich country will have a comparative advantage in the more capital-intensive commodity.

This conclusion resembles the familiar Heckscher–Ohlin proposition of trade theory, but the factors bringing about this conclusion are different. The important factor determining our conclusion is the relative difference in the economic lives of capital in the two sectors in the two countries. Suppose capital goods are more capital-intensive in production. Then we have shown above that, although the economic life of capital will be smaller in both the sectors of the

[6] If $r = g$,

$$\frac{H(T_c)}{H(T_m)} = \frac{e^{rT_c} - 1 - rT_c}{e^{rT_m} - 1 - rT_m}.$$

capital-rich country compared to that in the capital-poor country, the difference will be larger for the capital goods sector; and since in this model of fixed coefficients of production, both *ex ante* and *ex post*, productivity is inversely related to the length of the economic life of capital, one can see why the more capital-rich country will have a comparative advantage in producing the more capital-intensive capital goods. It may also be noted, in contrast to the standard Heckscher–Ohlin model, that although production functions *ex ante* are internationally identical, the extent of *utilization* of new technical knowledge in the industry as a whole is not the same in the different countries because of differences in the scrapping ages of machines.[7]

APPENDIX

We show here that $(G_1 + G_2)$ in (27) is positive or negative as T_m is larger or smaller than T_c.

From (16), (24), and (25),

$$\text{sign}[G_1 + G_2] = \text{sign}\left[\frac{\phi_{T_m}(r, T_m)}{\phi_r(r, T_m)} - \frac{\phi_{T_c}(r, T_c)}{\phi_r(r, T_c)}\right]. \tag{31}$$

If we define $x = \phi_{T_i}(r, T_i) > 0$ and $y = |\phi_r(r, T_i)| > 0$, $i = c, m$, the sign of the right-hand side of (31) depends on the sign of $[d(x/y)]/dT_i$, which is shown to be negative in this appendix. That means (31) is positive or negative as $T_m \gtrless T_c$. From (18)

$$x = \frac{g}{(r-g)}\,[e^{-gT_i} - e^{-rT_i}] \tag{32}$$

and

$$y = \frac{1}{r^2(r-g)^2}\,[(r-g)^2 + g(r-g)e^{-rT_i}(1 + rT_i)$$
$$+ r(ge^{-rT_i} - re^{-gT_i})] \tag{33}$$

[7] In this chapter we have compared two long-run equilibria with different values of r but the same value of g. If one allows g also to vary, that is, the two countries also differ in the rates of technical progress embodied in new machines, things become much more complicated. For an analysis of this case, see Bardhan [13], pp. 761–765.

From (32) and (33),

$$\frac{y}{x} = \frac{1}{gr^2(r-g)} \times \frac{[(r-g)^2 + g(r-g)e^{-rT_i}(1+rT_i) + r(ge^{-rT_i} - re^{-gT_i})]}{[e^{-gT_i} - e^{-rT_i}]}$$

$$= \frac{1}{gr^2(r-g)}\left[-r^2 + (r-g)g\,\frac{\{(\alpha-1)e^{\alpha z} + 1 + \alpha z - \alpha\}}{\{e^{(\alpha-1)z} - 1\}}\right], \qquad (34)$$

where $\alpha = r/g \neq 1$ and $z = gT_i$.

Defining

$$J(z) = \frac{(\alpha-1)e^{\alpha z} + 1 + \alpha z - \alpha}{e^{(\alpha-1)z}z - 1}$$

and differentiating $J(z)$ and dividing by $e^{(\alpha-1)z}$, we obtain

$$\operatorname{sign} J'(z) = \operatorname{sign}\{\alpha[e^{(1-\alpha)z} - 1][e^{\alpha z}(1-\alpha) - 1] - (1-\alpha)[(1-\alpha)e^{\alpha z} + \alpha - \alpha z - 1]\} \qquad (35)$$

If we call the expression on the right-hand side of (35) $V(z)$, then

$$V(0) = 0$$

and $V'(z) = \alpha(1-\alpha)[e^{\alpha z} - 1][e^{(1-\alpha)z} - 1] > 0$ for $\alpha \neq 1$. Therefore,

$$V(z) > 0 \qquad \text{for} \quad z > 0$$

or

$$J'(z) > 0.$$

Putting this in (34), we can say that y/x is an increasing function of T_i, or $[d(x/y)]/dT_i < 0$.

If $\alpha = 1$, that is, $r = g$, from (11a), (11b), and by integration of (17),

$$y = e^{-rT_i}\left[\frac{e^{rT_i} - 1}{r^2} - \frac{T_i}{r} - \frac{T_i^2}{2}\right]$$

and

$$x = rT_ie^{-rT_i}$$

so

$$\frac{y}{x} = \frac{1}{r^2}\left[\frac{e^{rT_i} - 1}{rT_i} - 1 - \frac{rT_i}{2}\right]$$

It can be easily confirmed that y/x is an increasing function of T_i.

PART TWO

Prescriptive Models

6

OPTIMUM INVESTMENT, TRADE, AND BORROWING IN AN OPEN ECONOMY

6.1. THE RAMSEY MODEL IN AN OPEN ECONOMY

In various parts of the preceeding chapters, particulaily in Chapters 3 and 4, whenever we discussed accumulation of capital we used specific types of savings functions as given from outside. However, a community's saving (and investment) decisions may be the product of an optimization process over time which involve economic choices as much as it involves ethical or political principles. Since Frank Ramsey's [78] pioneering article in 1928, the problem of optimum investment has fascinated a large number of economists. Until very recently very few of them discussed the problem in the context of an open economy.[1] This is part of a more general lack of any serious exercise in intertemporal welfare economics in the literature on international trade theory. In Part Two of this volume we discuss questions of optimum trade policy, investment and foreign borrowing, and

[1] The only such references we could cite from published literature are those of Bardhan [10], [15], Hamada [44], and Ryder [81].

exchange allocation in a framework that involves intertemporal choices on the part of society. We shall in general take the viewpoint of a government which is in a position to control the economy completely and to plan perfectly so as to maximize a given social welfare function over time.

This chapter has three sections: in Section 6.1 we extend the standard one-sector, closed-economy, Ramsey model to the case in which there is a consumer good and a capital good in an open economy and the rest of the world is static, and no foreign borrowing or lending takes place; in Section 6.2 we have the same model but without instantaneous balance of trade where intertemporal foreign borrowing or lending allows for balancing of trade only over the entire planning horizon.

For simplification we start with a case in which the labor force L in the economy—and hence by assumption the total population—is constant (without loss of generality, $L = 1$). The social welfare at any moment is taken to be a function of per capita consumption c only. The aim of the economy is to maximize the utility functional

$$\int_0^\infty e^{-\rho t} U[c(t)]\, dt,$$

where ρ is a constant and positive social rate of time discount. The utility function $U(c)$ is strictly concave and increasing. The planning horizon is infinite; as usual in this context, mathematical infinity is just a proxy for a "sufficiently long period." In the next two sections, as well as in Chapters 8 and 9, we consider finite planning horizons. On the one hand, the question of specifying an appropriate terminal stock for the finite-horizon planning model logically leads us toward the infinite horizon; on the other hand, as the planning horizon approaches infinity, the existence of an optimal policy may be difficult to guarantee. In this book we do not investigate the intricate questions of existence of optimal policy over an infinite horizon. If an optimal policy exists, the necessary conditions for optimality are the same whether the planning horizon is finite or infinite. Much of our attention in this part of the book will be devoted to an analysis of the implications of these necessary conditions for an optimum in each particular case. If the relevant Hamiltonian of the problem is concave (in state as well as control variables), any policy that satisfies the necessary conditions and the transversality conditions is optimal for the corresponding problem.

Per capita consumption is given by

$$c = F_c + z_c = f_c(k_c)l_c + z_c, \tag{1}$$

and per capita increase in capital stock by

$$\dot{k} = F_m + z_m = f_m(k_m)l_m + z_m, \tag{2}$$

where, as in Chapter 1, z_i is the per capita amount imported of the ith good, F_i is output of the ith good, k_i is the capital-labor ratio in ith sector, k is the total capital-labor ratio, $l_i = L_i/L$, and f_i is the output per unit of labor employed in the ith sector. As before, production in each sector is subject to constant returns to scale. The initial capital-labor ratio, $k(0)$, is given.

With full employment of capital and labor, as in (13) of Chapter 1,

$$k = k_c l_c + k_m(1 - l_c). \tag{3}$$

If foreign trade is always balanced,

$$z_c + Pz_m = 0, \tag{4}$$

where P, as before, is the world price of m with c as the *numéraire* good. If the home country has the ability to affect world prices, P is a function of z_m. For simplification we are assuming a static foreign country. In standard trade-theoretic terms, the home country faces a given foreign offer curve and if we superimpose this offer curve on our instantaneous domestic production-possibility curve, we obtain the usual Baldwin [5] envelope which summarizes the whole set of availabilities of the two goods open to the economy at any point in time. Our optimizing problem then is to maximize the social utility functional subject to the constraint embodied in the Baldwin envelope. For ensuring a maximum we assume that the Baldwin envelope is concave (a concave foreign offer curve[2] superimposed on a concave production-possibility curve gives a concave Baldwin envelope). Essentially the (interior) maximum will be given by the equality of the marginal rate of intertemporal substitution in consumption along the utility functional and the marginal rate of transformation indicated by the slope of the Baldwin envelope.

In deriving the maximizing conditions, we use the maximum

[2] The offer curve of a country relates z_c with z_m and its concavity implies $d^2z_c/dz_m^2 < 0$; this essentially means that a country has to export more and more to obtain one unit of import as its imports increase.

principle of Pontryagin et al. [78], particularly as interpreted by Arrow [3] in the context of optimum growth theory. Most of the time, especially in this chapter and the next, our attention is confined to the interior maximum, so that the more traditional techniques of the calculus of variations would give us the same results. The advantage of the maximum principle is that, apart from facilitating a systematic treatment of corner solutions in the case of inequality constraints on the control variables as in Chapters 8 and 9, it directly makes use of dual variables which have their natural interpretation of shadow prices.

If we here confine ourselves to only the interior solution of the optimizing problem, that is, when we are incompletely specialized in production of either good, consumption and investment, $1 > l_c > 0$, and from (1), (2), and (3),

$$\frac{f_c l_c}{P} > z_m > -f_m(1 - l_c).$$

Using (1), (2), and (3), the (generalized) Hamiltonian[3] H of the present problem is given by

$$He^{\rho t} = U(c) + \lambda[f_c(k_c)l_c - Pz_m - c] + q[f_m(k_m)(1 - l_c) + z_m], \qquad (5)$$

where λ and q are the imputed prices of the constraints (1) and (2), so that H is the present value of national income in terms of utility.

The necessary conditions for an interior maximum are that H is to be maximized with respect to the control variables[4] c, k_c, l_c and z_m, so that

$$\lambda = U'(c) \qquad (6)$$

$$\frac{q}{\lambda} = \frac{f_c'(k_c)}{f_m'(k_m)} \qquad (7)$$

$$\frac{f_c(k_c)}{f_c'(k_c)} - k_c = \frac{f_m(k_m)}{f_m'(k_m)} - k_m \qquad (8)$$

$$\frac{q}{\lambda} = P\left[1 + \frac{dP}{dz_m}\frac{z_m}{P}\right], \qquad (9)$$

[3] The $He^{\rho t}$ is Arrow's [3] "current-value" Lagrangean, which includes the standard Hamiltonian and the constraint function on control variables.

[4] k_m is not an independent control variable, since from (3) $k_m = (k - k_c l_c)/(1 - l_c)$.

and

$$\dot{q} = \rho q - \frac{\partial(He^{\rho t})}{\partial k} = q[\rho - f'_m(k_m)]. \tag{10}$$

Equation (6) implies that the imputed price of consumption is given by its marginal utility; (7) implies that the ratio of imputed prices is equalized to the marginal rate of domestic transformation of the two goods (given by the ratio of marginal products of capital in the two industries); (8) implies that the ratio of marginal product of labor to capital—we may call it w—is equalized between the two industries; (9) implies that the ratio of imputed prices is equalized to the marginal rate of transformation through foreign trade; (10) implies that the rate of growth in the imputed price of investment (indicating capital gains) is equal to the difference between own rate of interest (given by marginal productivity of capital in the capital-goods sector) and the rate of pure time preference: this is the fundamental equation of capital theory.

We might comment a little more on (9). The right-hand side of (9) gives the marginal rate of transformation through foreign trade which is in general different from the average rate of transformation given by P, the international price ratio, unless the country is small enough not to be able to affect the international price at all. From (17) in Chapter 1 we know that in international equilibrium $Z_m + \bar{Z}_m = 0$, where Z_m represents the total amount imported of m and the overbar denotes the foreign country. This immediately implies that

$$\frac{dP}{dz_m}\frac{z_m}{P} = \frac{1}{\dfrac{d\bar{Z}_m}{dP}\dfrac{P}{\bar{Z}_m}},$$

the reciprocal of the total price elasticity of supply of exports of capital goods by the foreign country (if the foreign country is an exporter of capital goods; if not, it is the reciprocal of the price elasticity of demand for imports of capital goods by the foreign country). Stated this way, (7) and (9) indicate the equality of domestic and foreign rates of transformation which is the familiar efficiency condition in the optimum tariffs literature.[5] When what is known as the optimum tariff (reckoned on the foreign price and at the rate

[5] See Graaff [40] and the literature cited there.

equal to the reciprocal of the price elasticity of supply of exports of capital goods by the foreign country) is levied (if the home country imports capital goods), the foreign rate of transformation is equalized to the domestic rate of transformation.

Given the necessary conditions and concavity of the Hamiltonian, the following transversality conditions are sufficient for optimality:

$$\lim_{t\to\infty} e^{-\rho t} q(t)k(t) = 0; \qquad \lim_{t\to\infty} q(t) \geq 0 \tag{11}$$

Given (1) to (11), it is now possible to fully characterize the optimum trajectory by analyzing the two differential equations (2) and (10). We shall refrain from a full characterization mainly because such analysis for the case of two differential equations is now familiar from the analysis of Uzawa [93], Cass [24], Ryder [81], and others, and also because there are very few trade-theoretic insights to be gained from the cumbersome calculations involved in characterizing the optimal path. In general the stationary solution of the two differential equations is a saddle point and the optimum path lies along its stable branches. If the initial capital-labor ratio $k(0)$ is small enough [strictly speaking, if $k(0) < k^*$, where k^* is the stationary capital-labor ratio which makes the own rate of interest equal to the rate of time preference], the home country's capital-labor ratio is increasing and q, the shadow price of investment is decreasing on the optimum path. Let us now briefly illustrate what this implies for terms of trade and imports (or exports) over time on the optimum path.

Let us call P^d the domestic price of m in terms of c, as given by the domestic rate of transformation in equation (7). We can show that P^d is a function of k and q alone. If for the purpose of our illustration we assume that the home country is for the time being an importer of capital-intensive capital goods (that is, $z_m > 0$, $k_m > k_c$) and that $(dP/z_m)(z_m/P)$ is a positive (that is, by importing more m we drive up its international price) constant, then we can show[6] that P^d is a

[6] From (1) and (4), $c = f_c(k_c)l_c - Pz_m(P)$. Since from (3), $l_c = (k - k_m)/(k_c - k_m)$, $\partial c/\partial k < 0$ for $k_m > k_c$. Since P^d is the relative domestic price of m in terms of c, under usual conditions output of c is a declining fuction of P^d so that

$$\frac{\partial(f_c l_c)}{\partial P^d} < 0.$$

decreasing function of k and an increasing function of q. This coupled with the result mentioned above that with $k(0) < k^*$, $\dot{k} > 0$ and $\dot{q} < 0$, implies that on the optimum path domestic price P^d is declining, so that from (9), terms of trade $(1/P)$ are improving and per capita imports of capital goods z_m declining over time.

We have so far assumed that the labor force in the home country is constant and also that the foreign country is static. The easiest way of relaxing these two assumptions is to take the case of labor growing at an exponential rate μ and assume that the foreign country is growing at a constant rate equal to μ. This assumption enables us to eliminate the effect of growth in the foreign country on variables in the home country in per capita terms. One can then use the same analysis as in our preceding discussion, except that if in our instantaneous utility function utility depends on per capita consumption alone (as contrasted with the case where the utility function of each generation is weighted by the size of that generation—the well-known Bentham–Meade utility function) then (10) changes into

$$\dot{q} = q[\rho + \mu - f'_m(k_m)] \tag{12}$$

Letting the foreign country grow in a more general way is a much more difficult problem. Economic growth in the foreign country will shift the shape and position of the foreign offer curve and hence that of the Baldwin envelope. Thus, growth in the foreign country introduces essentially the same type of problems as the phenomenon of continuous technical progress (which shifts the domestic production-possibility curve) in the closed-economy, optimum-growth models.

From (9),

$$P^d = P\left(1 + \frac{dP}{dz_m}\frac{z_m}{P}\right),$$

where

$$\frac{dP}{dz_m}\frac{z_m}{P}$$

is assumed to be a positive constant. All this means that $\partial c/\partial P^d < 0$. Now from (6) and (7), $U'(c)P^d - q = 0$. Since c is a function of k and q, this gives P^d as a function of k and q alone. With $\partial c/\partial k < 0$, $\partial c/\partial P^d < 0$ and with $U''(c) < 0$ it is easy to check that

$$\partial P^d/\partial k < 0 \qquad \text{and} \qquad \partial P^d/\partial q > 0.$$

6.2. INTERTEMPORAL BORROWING AND LENDING

In this section we examine the same problem as in the preceding section but with three changes: (i) we now have a finite planning horizon; (ii) instead of instantaneous balancing of trade as in (4) we now have trade balance only over the entire planning horizon with trade deficits and surpluses covered by borrowing from or lending abroad at a given rate of interest; and (iii) unlike in the preceding section we now assume that in the world market for capital goods m we are a small country, so that our buying or selling does not affect the world price of capital goods which we take as given at unity, whereas in the world market of consumer goods c we can affect the world price of c which we call P_c. Assumption (iii) may be important for those developing economies which are small importers of, say, machines, but large exporters of, say, some primary product.

Our aim is to maximize

$$\int_0^T U(c)e^{-\rho t}\,dt + k(T)e^{-\rho T}, \tag{13}$$

subject to (1), (2), (3), and the intertemporal trade balance equation

$$\int_0^T [P_c z_c + z_m]e^{-rt}\,dt = 0. \tag{14}$$

In (13) our maximand includes the discounted value of the terminal capital stock—the "scrap value" of capital in a generalized sense as used by Arrow [3] to represent some concern about the welfare of generations beyond our planning horizon T. Although we have taken a simple linear function, any general scrap-value function with a positive first derivative of $k(T)$ will suffice for the purpose of our present analysis.

As in most of the preceding section we assume, for simplification, a constant labor force $L = 1$. In (14) $[P_c z_c + z_m]$ is the total trade deficit (positive or negative) at any moment of time and r is the rate of interest (assumed constant) at which deficits can be covered by foreign borrowing or surpluses taken care of by foreign lending. It is important to analyze the implications of this intertemporal trade balance instead of the usual instantaneous trade balance, in view of the importance of foreign aid for most developing economies and in view of the plans of a number of them to be relatively independent of foreign aid by stipulated dates.

Equation (14) being an integral constraint, we have what is known as an "isoperimetric problem" in the literature on calculus of variations. The generalized Hamiltonian H of the present problem is given by

$$\begin{aligned} He^{\rho t} &= U(c) - \gamma e^{(\rho - r)t}[P_c z_c + z_m] + \lambda[f_c(k_c)l_c + z_c - c] \\ &\quad + q[f_m(k_m)(1 - l_c) + z_m], \end{aligned} \tag{15}$$

where γ is a constant, positive, and (as yet) undetermined Lagrange multiplier, λ and q are the imputed prices of the constraints (1) and (2), and H is accordingly the present value of national income in terms of utility.

The necessary conditions for an interior maximum are that H is to be maximized with respect to the control variables c, k_c, l_c, z_c, and z_m, so that

$$\lambda = U'(c) \tag{16}$$

$$\frac{q}{\lambda} = \frac{f_c'(k_c)}{f_m'(k_m)} \tag{17}$$

$$\frac{f_c(k_c)}{f_c'(k_c)} - k_c = \frac{f_m(k_m)}{f_m'(k_m)} - k_m \tag{18}$$

$$\lambda = \gamma e^{(\rho - r)t} P_c \left[1 + \frac{dP_c}{dz_c}\frac{z_c}{P_c}\right] \tag{19}$$

$$q = \gamma e^{(\rho - r)t} \tag{20}$$

and[7]

$$\dot{q} = \rho q - \frac{\partial(He^{\rho t})}{\partial k} = q[\rho - f_m'(k_m)]. \tag{21}$$

Conditions (16), (17), (18), and (21) are exactly the same as (6), (7), (8), and (10) in Section 6.1 and have exactly the same interpretation. Dividing (20) by (19), we obtain

$$\frac{q}{\lambda} = \frac{1}{P_c(1 + a)}, \tag{22}$$

[7] The undertermined multiplier γ is determined in the following way. From the transversality condition of the problem $q(T) = 1$ and so from (20) $\gamma = e(r - \rho)T$.

where

$$a = \frac{dP_c}{dz_c} \frac{zc}{P_c}$$

is the reciprocal of the price elasticity of demand for the exports of c in the rest of the world. Equation (22), like (9) in Section 6.1 implies that the ratio of imputed prices is equalized to the marginal rate of transformation through foreign trade. For simplification in the rest of this section, we assume a to be constant.

From (20) and (21), it immediately follows that

$$f'_m(k_m) = r, \tag{23}$$

or the own rate of interest in the home country is equalized to the world rate of interest. Since r, the rate of interest in the world market, is given, this implies that k_m and, from (18), k_c are constant; which in turn implies, from (17) and (16), that $q/[U'(c)]$ is a constant. From (22) this means P_c is a constant. Thus, if the home country faces a constant-elasticity export demand function and if it cannot affect the world rate of interest r, then on the optimum path its terms of trade and hence exports (or imports) of c should be constant.

Since k_c, k_m, and z_c are constant, and since from (3), $l_c = (k_m - k)/(k_m - k_c)$, from (1) we now can say that

$$\dot{c} = \frac{dc}{dk} \dot{k} = -\frac{f_c(k_c)\dot{k}}{k_m - k_c}. \tag{24}$$

Since $q/[U'(c)]$ is constant, from (20),

$$\frac{\dot{c}}{c} = \frac{r - \rho}{\theta(c)}, \tag{25}$$

where

$$\theta(c) = -\frac{U''(c)c}{U'(c)}$$

is the elasticity (positively defined) of the marginal utility of consumption.

From (24), (25), (2), and (3),

$$z_m = \frac{(\rho - r)c(k_m - k_c)}{\theta(c)f_c(k_c)} - \frac{f_m(k_m)(k - k_c)}{k_m - k_c}. \tag{26}$$

Since k_c, k_m, and z_c are constant, c is a function of k alone and hence in (26), z_m is also a function of k alone, so that

$$\dot{z}_m = \frac{dz_m}{dk}\dot{k} = -\dot{k}\left[\frac{f_m(k_m)}{k_m - k_c} + \frac{(\rho - r)}{\theta(c)}\left\{1 - \frac{c\theta'(c)}{\theta(c)}\right\}\right]. \tag{27}$$

Let us first take the case when $\rho > r$, (that is, the case in which society's time preference is higher than the marginal cost of borrowing). In this case, from (24), (25), and (27), $\dot{z}_m < 0$ if $k_m > k_c$ and $1 \geq [c\theta'(c)]/[\theta(c)]$. Since P_c and z_c are constant, this means that under the circumstances the trade deficit—which is equal to $[P_c z_c + z_m]$—is declining over time. From (14) this means that we start with a positive trade deficit (that is, positive borrowing) and gradually reduce our deficits until by the end of the planning horizon we pay off all the debts with trade surpluses.

If $\rho = r$, from (24), (25), and (27), z_m is constant. This means that $[P_c z_c + z_m]$ is constant over the entire planning horizon, which, from (14), implies that the trade is instantaneously balanced all the way over the planning period. In spite of the scope for borrowing, or lending, it does not pay because the time rate of discount is exactly equal to the marginal cost of (or return from) borrowing (or lending).

If $\rho < r$ with $k_m > k_c$ and $1 \geq [c\theta'(c)]/[\theta(c)]$, then using (18), (24), and (25) in (27), $\dot{z}_m > 0$ if $\theta \geq 1 - [c\theta'(c)]/[\theta(c)]$. In that case the trade deficit is increasing over time which, from (14), implies that we start with a negative trade deficit (that is, lending abroad) and gradually reduce our surplus until by the end of the planning horizon we incur deficits.

7

OPTIMUM TRADE POLICY IN A MODEL OF LEARNING BY DOING

7.1. LEARNING IN AN OPEN ECONOMY

In Chapter 6 we discussed some aspects of optimum investment trade and borrowing policies in models in which capital accumulation is a source of growth. In this chapter we ignore capital accumulation and consider a very simple dynamic model in which the volume of trade itself is an important determinant of growth of productivity. This is the case in which the economy "learns" by producing more exports or import substitutes, and cumulated experience enhances productivity.

One of the earliest instances of the incorporation of the concept of "learning by doing" in economic theory is the Hamilton–List infant-industry argument. It has been recognized in principle by John Stuart Mill and subsequent writers on international trade. As any elaboration of this idea involves some explicitly dynamic analysis, however, it has hardly been integrated into the main corpus of trade theory which is mostly comparative-static in nature; until recently, it has received nothing more than nodding recognition as just one of the few "exceptions" to the doctrine of free trade. In this chapter we analyze the optimum extent and time path of protection of the learning industry, whereas usual analysis stops at merely pointing out the need for protection in such cases.

We have two goods c and m that use capital K and labor L in production under constant returns to scale. The learning effect that increases productivity of factors depends on the cumulated volume of *output* in an industry.[1] Since the infant-industry argument is based (at least implicitly) on some kind of differential learning effect, we assume, for simplicity, that learning is operative only in one of the industries, say, in industry m. The production functions are:

$$F_c = F_c(K_c, L_c) = L_c f_c(k_c) \tag{1}$$

$$F_m = Q^n L_m f_m(k_m), \tag{2}$$

where F_i is the current rate of output and k_i the capital-labor ratio employed in ith industry; $i = c, m$; Q is the cumulated volume of output of m so that $\dot{Q} = dQ/dt = F_m$ (we shall, later in this section, alter this assumption slightly by introducing a term for depreciation of experience); Q^n incorporates the effect of learning or experience on productivity (we assume $1 > n > 0$);[2] the way we have introduced the learning term also implies our simplifying assumption that the

[1] Arrow in his celebrated model of learning by doing [2] takes cumulated gross investment as the stock of experience affecting productivity. While this idea is useful in the context of an aggregative growth model such as Arrow's, for studying the phenomenon of learning at the industry level it seems more appropriate to take the cumulated volume of industry output as the index of productivity-raising experience. At any rate, most of the empirical evidence of learning in production of airframes, machine tools, and so on, relates to the cumulated volume of industry output. See, for example, Hirsch [46].

[2] This, of course, is a very special kind of learning function that is similar to the empirically observed exponential learning function for airframes. Most of our subsequent results, however, carry through (with one exception noted in footnote (17), if, instead, we take a more general learning function so that $F_m = G(Q)L_m f_m(k_m)$ with $G'(Q) > 0$ and $G''(Q) < 0$. The assumption about the derivatives of the $G(Q)$ function means that learning enhances productivity but at a diminishing rate.

In formalizing the infant-industry concept, however, a more suitable learning function might be one where $G(Q)$ reaches an upper bound $\overline{G}$ for a finite Q, where $\overline{G}$ is a measure of the rest of the world's efficiency level (the thing to be "caught up"). In Section 7.3 we explore the implications of such a learning function.

productivity-enhancing effect of learning is neutral with respect to the two factors of production.[3] The stock of experience for the industry is under the control of no single firm; it is an irreversible external economy to it.[4]

As in (14) of Chapter 1, the amount imported Z_i of the ith good is determined by domestic demand and supply conditions, so that $Z_i = D_i - F_i$, $i = c, m$, where D_i is the amount demanded of the ith good. Since we want to concentrate on the operation of the learning effect, we assume in this chapter that the total supply of labor and capital in the economy is given. Without further loss of generality, we take $L = 1$. So, with the use of (1) and (2) we can now write

$$D_c = f_c(_c)l_c + z_c \tag{3}$$

$$D_m = Q^n f_m(k_m)(1 - l_c) + z_m, \tag{4}$$

where, as before, $l_c = L_c/L$, and z_i is the per capita amount imported of the ith good. If we assume balance of trade,

$$z_c + \bar{P} z_m = 0, \tag{5}$$

where $\bar{P}$ is the international price of m in terms of c. For simplicity we assume in this chapter that ours is a small country in a large world, so that the international price $\bar{P}$ is given (this helps one to isolate the considerations of the infant-industry argument from those of the standard optimum tariff argument). For the time being we are assuming the rest of the world to be static. It would be more realistic to have continuous learning going on in the rest of the world as well, however, possibly changing the international price level. We consider this case in Section 7.4.

The equation for accumulation of experience (which increases productivity in industry m) is given by

$$\dot{Q} = F_m - \delta Q \tag{6}$$

In other words, our stock of experience Q in industry m increases by

[3] Most of the empirical studies on learning concentrate on the inverse relationship between unit *labor* costs and cumulated volume of output. Wright [94], in his original study of learning functions for airframes, however, observed learning effects for other inputs as well.

[4] That the basic rationale for the infant-industry argument is provided by such irreversible external economies is now well recognized. See Meade [64], p. 256, Kemp [54], p. 187. For a number of concrete examples of such external economies, see Bardhan [7].

the current rate of production in that industry *net* of depreciation[5] of experience ("forgetting") at rate δ.

Let us suppose that the social objective is to maximize

$$\int_0^\infty U(D_c, D_m)e^{-\rho t}\,dt,$$

where U is the instantaneous utility function assumed to be strictly concave and having positive marginal utilities, and ρ is the positive social rate of discount.

For a full solution of the optimizing problem we have to discuss a number of patterns of specialization (specialization in consuming c, in consuming m, in producing c, in producing m, consumption of both m and c, production of both m and c, and so on). As before, in order to economize space we confine ourselves to only the interior case—in which we produce and consume both commodities—the case which is usually the most interesting. This means

$$F_c > 0 \quad \text{and} \quad F_m > 0 \tag{7}$$

$$D_c > 0 \quad \text{and} \quad D_m > 0. \tag{8}$$

Equations (3), (4), (5), and (8) imply that

$$-Q^n f_m(k_m)(1 - l_c) < z_m < \frac{f_c(k_c)l_c}{\bar{P}}. \tag{9}$$

Equation (7) implies, assuming labor to be essential to production, that

$$1 > l_c > 0. \tag{10}$$

The Hamiltonian H of the present problem is given by

$$\begin{aligned} He^{\rho t} = {} & U(D_c, D_m) + \lambda[f_c(k_c)l_c - \bar{P}z_m - D_c] \\ & + \mu[f_m(k_m)(1 - l_c)Q^n + z_m - D_m] \\ & + \gamma[Q^n f_m(k_m)(1 - l_c) - \delta Q], \end{aligned} \tag{11}$$

[5] Although this is assumed for mathematical simplification, some motivation may be given for this depreciation of experience. For example, in an underdeveloped country an important part of learning is adaptation to industrial employment on the part of the worker from a rural area and this is lost when he leaves the labor force. For those who find this assumption of depreciation of experience still not very appealing, we have worked out a case without this assumption in Section 7.4.

where λ, μ, and γ are imputed prices of the constraints (3), (4), and (6), respectively, with (5) substituted in (3) and (2) substituted in (6); λ and μ are the demand prices for consumption of c and m, respectively, and γ is the imputed price of productivity-enhancing experience. H can, therefore, be interpreted to be the present value of national income in terms of utility.

The necessary conditions for maximum are as follows:

$$\lambda = \frac{\partial U}{\partial D_c} \tag{12}$$

$$\mu = \frac{\partial U}{\partial D_m} \tag{13}$$

$$\frac{\mu}{\lambda} = \bar{P} \tag{14}$$

$$\frac{\mu + \gamma}{\lambda} = \frac{f_c'(k_c)}{f_m'(k_m)Q^n} \tag{15}$$

$$\frac{f_c(k_c)}{f_c'(k_c)} - k_c = \frac{f_m(k_m)}{f_m'(k_m)} - k_m \tag{16}$$

$$\dot{\gamma} = (\rho + \delta)\gamma - (\mu + \gamma)f_m(k_m)(1 - l_c)nQ^{n-1}. \tag{17}$$

Equation (14) implies that the ratio of marginal utilities in consumption should be equalized to the given international price ratio. The right-hand side of (15) gives[6] the marginal rate of domestic transformation. Equation (16) implies that the ratio of marginal products of labor to capital—which we might call w—should be equalized between the two industries. Equation (17) gives us the optimum rate of change in the shadow price of experience.

Given these necessary conditions the transversality condition sufficient for optimality is

$$\lim_{t \to \infty} \gamma Q e^{-\rho t} = 0, \qquad \lim_{t \to \infty} \gamma \geq 0 \tag{18}$$

In Section 7.2 we analyze in detail the implications of these optimality conditions. Before we do that, however, let us simplify

[6] In deriving (15) and (16), we have used the full-employment equation (3) of Chapter 1 whereby $1 - l_c = (k_c - k)/k_c - k_m$, as we have noted in (23) of Chapter 1.

the problem by introducing a rather strong assumption. We assume that the instantaneous utility function $U(D_c, D_m)$ is homogeneous of degree one (that is, the income elasticity of demand for either good is unity). This means that in (12) and (13) λ and μ depend only on D_c/D_m, the ratio of consumption of the two goods. Then, from (14) this ratio is constant so that λ and μ become constant. Without this drastic simplification of the utility function, the problem is much more complicated to analyze, although solvable in principle.

7.2. THE OPTIMALITY CONDITIONS

If we define[7]

$$A(w) = \frac{f_c'[k_c(w)]}{f_m'[k_m(w)]}$$

and

$$P^d = \frac{A(w)}{Q^n},$$

we can rewrite (15) as

$$\frac{\mu + \gamma}{\lambda} = \frac{A(w)}{Q^n} = P^d \tag{19}$$

P^d is the marginal rate of domestic transformation, while $\bar{P}$ is the marginal rate of transformation through foreign trade as well as the marginal rate of substitution in consumption. Unless the government intervenes, competitive producers of m will produce according to the market price $\bar{P}(=\mu/\lambda)$ and there will be underproduction of m from the social point of view. In order to attain the social optimum, the government should assure the producers a price equal to P^d $[=(\mu + \gamma)/\lambda]$. The optimum rate of subsidy to the learning industry[8] is given by $\bar{P}(1 + \tau) = P^d$, or $\tau = \gamma/\mu$, where τ is the rate of subsidy per unit of output. As long as experience increases productivity, its

[7] If we call w the ratio of marginal product of labor to capital, then we can use (16) to derive k_i as a unique function of w as in (9) of Chapter 1 and Figure 1.1.

[8] It may be a mixture of tax on the nonlearning industry and subsidy to the learning industry.

imputed price γ is positive[9] and so is the rate of subsidy τ. Two points are important to note here. (a) As is by now well recognized (see, for example, Bhagwati and Ramaswami [20]), a subsidy is better than a tariff in such cases because the latter in restoring the equality between domestic and foreign marginal rates of transformation also drives a wedge between the marginal rate of consumer substitution and that of transformation. (b) It should be noted that good m may be imported or exported, although we have assumed some limits on both sides as implied in (9). So our prescribed subsidization of learning may involve a subsidy to the import-competing industry or to the export industry, as the case may be.

One of the main purposes of this chapter is to determine the time pattern of the optimum subsidy, that is, the nature of $\dot{\tau}$ over time.

Let us for this purpose take the two differential equations of our model given by (6) and (17).

$$\dot{Q} = Q^n B(w) - \delta Q \tag{20}$$

$$\dot{\gamma} = (\rho + \delta)\gamma - (\mu + \gamma)B(w)nQ^{n-1}, \tag{21}$$

where

$$B(w) = f_m[k_m(w)][1 - l_c(w)].$$

Now from (19), w can be written as a function of P^d and Q. So (20) may be rewritten as

$$\dot{Q} = \phi(Q, P^d). \tag{22}$$

Since μ and λ are constant, from (19) and (21),

$$\dot{P}^d = \frac{\dot{\gamma}}{\lambda} = \frac{\gamma}{\lambda}\left[(\rho + \delta) - \left(1 - \frac{\mu}{\gamma}\right)nQ^{n-1}B(w)\right]. \tag{23}$$

Since w is a function of P^d and Q, and γ is a function of P^d alone, we can rewrite (23) as

$$\dot{P}^d = \Psi(Q, P^d). \tag{24}$$

As explained in detail in Appendix 1, under the sufficient condition of $[\partial F_m/\partial Q][Q/F_m]$ (given P^d)—or what might be called the "learning

[9] This follows from (15), (17), and (18).

elasticity of output" of m—being less than unity, the stationary solution (Q_*, P_*^d) to the two differential equations (22) and (24) is unique and is also a saddle point, as is indicated in Figure 7.1. Under

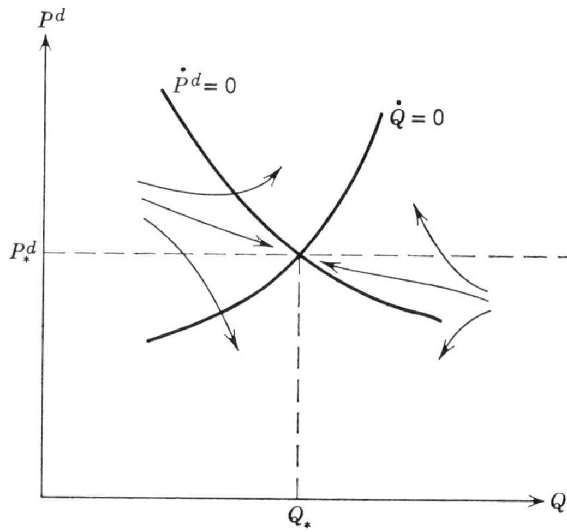

Figure 7.1

the same sufficient condition, the $\dot{Q} = 0$ curve is uniformly upward-sloping for the (interior) region we are considering. Under a stronger sufficient condition of the price elasticity of output of m being small enough,[10] the $\dot{P}^d = 0$ curve is uniformly downward-sloping in the region we are considering.

Given our transversality condition (18), if $Q(0) = Q_*$, the unique optimum path is indicated by the singular solution (Q_*, P_*^d) and the optimum rate of subsidy to the learning industry,

$$\tau_* = \frac{P_*^d - \bar{P}}{\bar{P}} = \frac{n\delta}{\rho + (1-n)\delta},$$

a constant. If, however, $Q(0) \neq Q_*$, the optimum path of (Q, P^d)

[10] In the context of developing economies (where the infant-industry argument is supposed to apply with particular relevance) this assumption may not be inappropriate, since such economies are usually characterized by low substitution elasticities in production (low "capacity to transform" in Kindleberger's terms).

lies along the stable branches of the saddle point given the transversality condition. It can be seen from Figure 7.1 that along the optimum path, *if* $Q(0) < Q_*$ (that is, the initial stock of experience is small enough), Q steadily increases and P^d steadily decreases to asymptotically approach the stationary solution (Q_*, P^d_*), and therefore the optimum rate of subsidy τ steadily decreases to asymptotically approach the stationary rate τ_*. If, on the other hand, $Q(0) > Q_*$, by similar reasoning the optimum rate of subsidy steadily increases to asymptotically approach the stationary rate τ_*.[11]

7.3. TEMPORARY LEARNING

In Section 7.2 we characterized the time path of the optimum rate of subsidy to the learning industry in this model: if the initial stock of experience is small, the optimum rate of subsidy steadily decreases over time to asymptotically approach a stationary rate that is positive. The subsidy always remains positive because with the learning function incorporated in (2), experience always enhances productivity, and with the spillover of benefits of the learning process to all firms[12] there tends to be an underproduction of m from the social point of view if the industry is not subsidized. Much of the usual infant-industry argument is concerned with *temporary* protection, however, where the learning process is more in the nature of overcoming a historical handicap, a matter of catching up with a foreign country's efficiency level, that that of a continuous productivity-enhancing phenomenon, and the subsidy is to be removed as soon as the "infant" becomes an adult. The implications of this kind of a

[11] We are assuming that at the stationary solution the economy is incompletely specialized. In this model, since learning occurs only in industry m and since international prices are given, the economy tends toward complete specialization in m. A sufficient condition for avoiding it is to assume that $\bar{P} < [A(w_{\max})]/Q^n_*$, where

$$w_{\max} = \frac{f_m(k)}{f_m'(k)} - k.$$

[12] There are some types of learning processes the benefits of which are specific to the learning firm, and in such cases, obviously, the case for subsidy should not arise.

learning process can, however, be discussed retaining a large part of the analytic framework outlined in earlier sections of this paper.

Let us rewrite (2) as

$$F_m = G(Q)L_m f_m(k_m), \tag{25}$$

where G is the learning function, $G(0)$ is a constant, $G'(Q) > 0$, $G''(Q) < 0$ for Q less than a finite positive level of $\bar{Q}$, and for $Q \geq \bar{Q}$, $G(Q) = \bar{G}$, a constant.[13] This means that the stock of experience enhances productivity (at a diminishing rate) up to a point, and then at a certain level of experience $\bar{Q}$ the country catches up with the foreign efficiency level $\bar{G}$, and there is no more learning.

How will this affect our analysis of the time path of the optimum rate of subsidy? As long as $Q < \bar{Q}$, both the $\dot{Q} = 0$ and $\dot{P}^d = 0$ curves will be of the same shape as before, if one makes the same assumptions. The imputed price of experience γ will be positive as long as $Q < \bar{Q}$, but for $Q \geq \bar{Q}$, $\gamma = 0$, implying the completion of the learning process. The rate of subsidy τ being equal to γ/μ is therefore zero for $Q \geq \bar{Q}$. So if the $\dot{Q} = 0$ and $\dot{P}^d = 0$ curves do not intersect for $Q < \bar{Q}$, then the optimum rate of subsidy τ steadily declines over time until it reaches zero at $Q = \bar{Q}$. If the $\dot{Q} = 0$ and $\bar{P}^d = 0$ curves intersect before Q reaches $\bar{Q}$, the conclusion of Section 7.2 remains valid for the case in which the initial stock of experience is small enough.

7.4. LEARNING IN BOTH COUNTRIES

In this section we revert to the case of continuous learning but consider the relaxation of two other assumptions in the model. One of our assumptions has been to consider the rest of the world as static. A more interesting model might be one in which learning by doing is continuously going on abroad as well as in the home country. This means that even if ours is a small country in a large world we may no longer take the international price $\bar{P}$ as static. $\bar{P}$ may now change because of learning in the rest of the world. Once we introduce learning abroad, we shall, of course, have to assume something about the transferability of the benefits of that learning.

[13] We assume that at the point when $Q = \bar{Q}$, $G'(Q) = 0$ and $G''(Q) = 0$.

In other words, we have to consider the *international* external economies of the learning process. In this section we shall assume that an increase in the stock of experience in the world outside will costlessly enhance the productivity[14] in our small country as well. In the process of working out the implications of this factor, we shall also do away with another possibly restrictive assumption from our preceding three sections, namely, that of positive depreciation of experience.

In order to simplify our calculations, we assume that the stock of experience $\bar{Q}$ in the rest of the world for industry m is growing at a constant rate α and also that the international price of m, $\bar{P}$, is, as a consequence, declining at the rate α. The production function of m in the home country is now given by

$$F_m = G(Q, \bar{Q}) L_m f_m(k_m), \tag{26}$$

where G is the neutral productivity function, which is increasing (at a diminishing rate) for both Q and $\bar{Q}$. For simplicity we assume that the $G(Q, \bar{Q})$ function is homogeneous of degree one so that

$$G(Q, \bar{Q}) = \bar{Q} g(x), \tag{27}$$

where $x = Q/\bar{Q}$.

We also make a further simplifying assumption regarding the utility function $U(D_c, D_m)$. In Section 7.1 we took U as homogeneous of degree one; for simplification, we shall now take U to be in the more specific Cobb–Douglas form:

$$U(D_c, D_m) = D_c^{\beta} D_m^{1-\beta}, \tag{28}$$

where β is a positive constant.

Armed with these simplifying assumptions, we are now ready to tackle our learning model, which is otherwise much more general than the one in preceding sections.

The international price of m, $\bar{P}$, is now declining at a constant rate α, so that in comparison to (14) we now have

$$\frac{\mu(t)}{\gamma(t)} = \bar{P}(0) e^{-\rho t}. \tag{29}$$

[14] This is, of course, an extreme assumption of free transferability of knowledge across countries (apart from problems of adaption of foreign technology to the specific pattern of available resources, factor prices, market possibilities, and so on, in the home country).

As shown in Appendix 2, it is easy to derive from (12), (13), (28), and (29) that

$$\lambda(t) = \lambda(0)e^{\alpha(1-\beta)t} \tag{30}$$

and

$$\mu(t) = \mu(0)e^{-\alpha\beta t}. \tag{31}$$

Without loss of generality we take $\lambda(0) = \mu(0) = \bar{P}(0) = \bar{Q}(0) = 1$. Comparing with (19), the marginal rate of domestic transformation is now given by

$$P^d = \frac{\mu\ t) + \gamma(t)}{\lambda(t)} = \frac{A(w)}{G(Q, \bar{Q})}, \tag{32}$$

Since $\bar{Q}$ is growing at rate α, we can rewrite (32), with the help of (27) and (29), as

$$\frac{A(w)}{g(x)} = 1 + \gamma(t)e^{\alpha\beta t} = 1 + y(t), \tag{33}$$

where $y(t) = \gamma(t)e^{\alpha\beta t}$.

In Section 7.2 we saw that $\tau = [\gamma(t)]/[\mu(t)]$. From (31), this means $\tau = y(t)$. We shall be interested in finding the optimum time path of $y(t)$.

As explained in Appendix 2 under the sufficient condition of $(\partial F_m/\partial Q)(Q/F_m)$—or what might be called the elasticity of output with respect to domestic learning—being less than unity, the stationary solution (x_*, y_*) to the differential equations governing the motion of x and y is unique and is also a saddle point. Under the same sufficient condition, the $\dot{x} = 0$ curve is uniformly upward-sloping, and under a stronger sufficient condition of the price elasticity of supply of m being small enough, the $\dot{y} = 0$ curve is uniformly downward-sloping for the (interior) region we are considering. The phase diagram looks *exactly* as in Figure 7.1 when Q is replaced by x and P^d by y.[15]

If $x(0) = x_*$, the unique optimum path is indicated by the singular

[15] We assume that the social rate of discount is high enough so that $\rho > (1 - \beta)\alpha$. This is needed to satisfy the transversality condition (18).

solution (x_*, y_*), and the optimum rate of subsidy to the learning industry,[16]

$$\tau_* = y_* = \frac{\alpha g'(x_*)x_*}{g(x_*)[\rho + \alpha\beta] - \alpha g'(x_*)x_*}.$$

If, however, $x(0) \neq x_*$, the optimum path of (x, y) lies along the stable branches of the saddle point. If the home country's initial stock of experience is small enough, so that $x(0) < x_*$, along the optimum path y, and therefore the optimum rate of subsidy τ, steadily decreases to asymptotically approach the stationary rate τ_*. If, on the other hand, $x(0) > x_*$, the optimum rate of subsidy steadily increases to asymptotically approach the stationary rate τ_*.

APPENDIX 1

Taking our two differential equations (22) and (24), from (20) and (22),

$$\left(\frac{\partial \phi}{\partial Q}\right)_{\phi=0} = Q^n \frac{dB(w)}{dw}\frac{\partial w}{\partial Q} - Q^{n-1}B(w)(1-n), \tag{34}$$

where

$$B(w) = f_m[k_m(w)]\frac{[k_c(w) - k]}{[k_c(w) - k_m(w)]}$$

and $Q^n B = \rho Q$ when $\phi = 0$. Now the "learning elasticity of output" of m is

$$\frac{\partial F_m}{\partial Q}\frac{Q}{F_m} = n + \frac{Q}{B(w)}\left[\frac{dB(w)}{dw}\frac{\partial w}{\partial Q}\right]. \tag{35}$$

If this elasticity is less than unity, (34) is obviously negative. Let us determine sufficient conditions for this elasticity to be less than unity.

Let e_s be the price elasticity of output of m, so that using the value

[16] That the stationary rate τ_* is positive can be shown as follows. Since under our assumption in footnote 15 $\rho > (1 - \beta)\alpha$, the denominator in the expression for y_* is larger than $\alpha[g(x_*) - g'(x_*)x_*]$, which is positive since the bracketed expression is equal to the marginal contribution to domestic output from a rise in the stock of experience abroad.

of $\partial w/\partial P^d$ from (19), and using (11) and (12) of Chapter 1 to obtain $A'(w)$,

$$e_s = \frac{\partial F_m}{\partial P^d}\frac{P^d}{F_m} = Q^n B'(w)\frac{\partial w}{\partial P^d}\frac{P^d}{F_m} = \frac{B'(w)}{B(w)}\frac{A(w)}{A'(w)} > 0 \qquad (36)$$

where $A(w)$ is defined as in (19).

Now using the value of $\partial w/\partial Q$ from (19), (35) can be rewritten as

$$\frac{\partial F_m}{\partial Q}\frac{Q}{F_m} = n\left[1 + \frac{B'(w)}{B(w)}\frac{A(w)}{A'(w}\right] = n(1 + e_s). \qquad (37)$$

Thus the learning elasticity of output being less than unity implies that

$$n(1 + e_s) < 1. \qquad (38)$$

For example, if the price elasticity of output of m is less than or equal to unity, a learning coefficient n, equal to or less than 0.5, is sufficient for (34) to be negative.

If (34) is negative, and since with price elasticity of output of m positive, $\partial\phi/\partial P^d = \partial F_m/\partial P^d > 0$, we can now say that

$$\left(\frac{dP^d}{dQ}\right)_{\phi=0} = -\left[\frac{\partial\phi}{\partial Q}\Big/\frac{\partial\phi}{\partial P^d}\right]_{\phi=0} > 0 \qquad (39)$$

so that $\dot{Q} = 0$ curve is upward-sloping as in Figure 7.1. From (19), (23), and (24).

$$\left(\frac{\partial\psi}{\partial Q}\right)_{\psi=0} = -\left[nQ^{n-2}(n-1)B(w) + nQ^{n-1}\frac{dB(w)}{dw}\frac{\partial w}{\partial Q}\right]P^d. \qquad (40)$$

From (35), once again, if the learning elasticity of output of m is less than unity, (40) is positive.[17]

From (19), (23), (24), and (36) and since μ and λ are constant,

$$\left(\frac{\partial\psi}{\partial P^d}\right)_{\psi=0} = nQ^{n-1}\left[B\frac{\mu}{\gamma} - P^d\frac{dB(w)}{dw}\frac{\partial w}{\partial P^d}\right] = nQ^{n-1}B\left[\frac{\mu}{\gamma} - e_s\right]. \qquad (41)$$

[17] If instead of having the special learning function $G(Q) = Q^n$, $1 > n > 0$, we have a more general learning function $G(Q)$ with $G'(Q) > 0$, $G''(Q) < 0$, we have to assume the following for (40) to be positive:

$$\frac{G'(Q)Q}{G(Q)} - \frac{G''(Q)Q}{G'(Q)} \geq 1.$$

Without some extra assumptions it does not seem to be possible to be unambiguous about the sign of (41) in general. All we can say is that if the price elasticity of output of m, e_s, is small enough, (41) will be positive.[18] In that case,

$$\left(\frac{dP^d}{dQ}\right)_{\psi=0} = -\left[\frac{\partial\psi}{\partial Q}\Big/\frac{\partial\psi}{\partial P^d}\right]_{\psi=0} < 0. \tag{42}$$

So under our assumptions the $\dot{P}^d = 0$ curve is downward-sloping as in Figure 7.1.

Given the shapes of the $\dot{Q} = 0$ and $\dot{P}^d = 0$ curves under our assumptions, the stationary solution is unique. For proving uniqueness or the saddle-point property of our stationary solution, however, the last assumption we have just made, namely, that the price elasticity of output of m is small enough, is not really necessary. Let us show why.

Although we cannot be unambiguous about the sign of

$$\left(\frac{\partial\psi}{\partial P^d}\right)_{\psi=0}$$

in general without this extra assumption, we can show that around the stationary equilibrium point, (Q_*, P^d_*), we know its sign without that assumption. From (20) and (23), when $\dot{Q} = 0$ and $\dot{P}^d = 0$,

$$1 + \frac{\mu}{\gamma_*} = \frac{\rho + \delta}{B(w)_* n Q_*^{n-1}} = \frac{\rho + \delta}{n\delta}.^{19} \tag{43}$$

Using (43) in (41),

$$\left(\frac{\partial\psi}{\partial P^d}\right)_{\substack{\psi=0\\ \phi=0}} = B(w)_* Q_*^{n-1} \frac{[\rho + \delta\{1 - n(1 + e_s)\}]}{\delta}. \tag{44}$$

Equation (44) is positive under our earlier assumption that the learning elasticity of output of m is less than unity, as may be checked

[18] An alternative sufficient condition is $1 > \tau e_s$, since $\tau = \gamma/\mu$. So if the price elasticity of output of m is less than or equal to unity and $\tau(0)$ is less than 100%, (41) is positive.

[19] This implies that

$$\tau_* = \frac{\gamma_*}{\mu} = \frac{n\delta}{\rho + (1 - n)\delta}.$$

from (38). Thus, around the stationary equilibrium the $\dot{P}^d = 0$ curve must be downward-sloping and the stationary solution is unique, since $\dot{Q} = 0$ is always upward-sloping. Expanding the two differential equations (22) and (24) around the point (Q_*, P_*^d) and using (34), (35), (36), (40), and (44), we can see that under our assumption that the learning elasticity of output of m is less than unity, the characteristic roots of the resulting linear system are real and opposite in sign, indicating that the stationary solution is a saddle point.

We need the extra assumption that e_s is small enough to ensure that not merely around the point (Q_*, P_*^d) but

$$\left(\frac{\partial\psi}{\partial P^d}\right)_{\psi=0} > 0$$

in general throughout the region we are considering. This ensures the result that for $Q(0) < Q_*$, τ *steadily* decreases.

APPENDIX 2

From (28),

$$\lambda = \beta d^{\beta-1} \qquad \text{and} \qquad \mu = (1-\beta)d^{\beta}, \tag{45}$$

where $d = D_c/D_m$.

Using (45) in (29), $\dot{d}/d = -\alpha$, and that immediately implies (30) and (31).

Let us now analyze the new differential equations of our system. The analysis of the properties of these differential equations is nearly the same as that of our earlier differential equations (22) and (24) analyzed in Appendix 1. We shall, therefore, be very brief here.

Since we are no longer assuming depreciation of experience, (20) is to be rewritten, with the use of (26) and (27), as

$$\dot{Q} = F_m = \bar{Q}g(x)B(w). \tag{46}$$

Since

$$x = Q/\bar{Q},\ \dot{x} = \dot{Q}/\bar{Q} - \alpha x. \tag{47}$$

From (33), w is only a function of x and y. Using $\dot{Q}$ from (46), (47) may now be rewritten as

$$\dot{x} = B(w)g(x) - \alpha x = \phi(x, y). \tag{48}$$

As in (34), if the elasticity of output with respect to domestic learning, that is,

$$\frac{\partial F_m}{\partial Q}\frac{Q}{F_m} = \frac{g'(x)x}{g(x)} + \frac{B'(w)x}{B(w)}\frac{\partial w}{\partial x}x$$

is less than unity, then

$$(\phi_x)_{\dot{x}=0} < 0.$$

From (33), (36), and (48),

$$\phi_y = g(x)B'(w)\frac{\partial w}{\partial x} = g^2\frac{B'(w)}{A'(w)} > 0. \tag{49}$$

This means that

$$\left(\frac{dy}{dx}\right)_{\dot{x}=0} = -\frac{\phi_x}{\phi_y} > 0, \tag{50}$$

or, the $\dot{x} = 0$ curve is upward-sloping in (x, y) space. With our new production function for m as denoted by (26) and (27), (21) must be rewritten as

$$\dot{\gamma} = \rho\gamma - (\mu + \gamma)g'(x)B(w). \tag{51}$$

From (33),

$$\frac{\dot{y}}{y} = \alpha\beta + \frac{\dot{\gamma}}{\gamma}. \tag{52}$$

Since $(\mu + \gamma)/\gamma = 1 + (1/y)$, (52) can be rewritten as

$$\dot{y} = y(\rho + \alpha\beta) - [1 + y]g'(x)B(w) = \psi(x, y). \tag{53}$$

From (53),

$$\psi_x = -[1 + y]\left[B(w)g''(x) + g'(x)B'(w)\frac{\partial w}{\partial x}\right]. \tag{54}$$

As in Appendix 1, (54) is positive (since $g'' < 0$) if the price elasticity of output of m is small enough or, alternatively, if[20]

$$\frac{g'(x)x}{g(x)} - \frac{g''(x)x}{g'(x)} \geq 1.$$

[20] If we assume a special form of the $G(Q, \bar{Q})$ function, namely, $G(Q, \bar{Q}) = Q^n\bar{Q}^{1-n}$, $1 > n > 0$. Then it is easy to show that

$$\frac{g'(x)x}{g(x)} - \frac{g''(x)x}{g'(x)} = 1.$$

From (53),

$$(\psi_y)_{\dot{y}=0} = \frac{g'(x)}{y}\left[B(w) - y(1 + y)B'(w)\frac{\partial w}{\partial y}\right]. \tag{55}$$

As in (41) in Appendix 1, (55) is positive if the price elasticity of output of m is small enough.

Thus

$$\left(\frac{dy}{dx}\right)_{\dot{y}=0} = -\frac{\psi_x}{\psi_y} < 0 \tag{56}$$

or, under our assumptions the $\dot{y} = 0$ curve is downward-sloping in (x, y) space.

Given the shapes of the $\dot{x} = 0$ and $\dot{y} = 0$ curves the stationary solution is a unique saddle point. However, as in Appendix 1, for proving uniqueness or the saddle-point property of the stationary solution the assumption of price elasticity of output of m being small enough for (55) to be positive is not really necessary. The proof of this statement follows exactly the same kind of proof for a similar statement concerning the stationary solution in Appendix 1 and hence is omitted here. We need the assumption referring to the price elasticity of output of m being small enough for (55) to be positive in order to ensure that the $\dot{y} = 0$ curve is downward-sloping, not merely around the stationary equilibrium point (x_*, y_*), but in general throughout the region we are considering. This ensures the result that for $x(0) < x_*$, y steadily decreases over time.

The stationary rate of subsidy τ_* can easily be calculated by putting (48) and (53) equal to zero. From (48) and (53),[21]

$$\tau_* = y_* = \frac{\alpha g'(x_*)x_*}{g(x_*)[\rho + \alpha\beta] - \alpha g'(x_*)x_*}.$$

[21] If we take the special form of the $G(Q, \bar{Q})$ function as in footnote 20, then

$$\tau_* = \frac{\alpha n}{\rho + \alpha(\beta - n)}.$$

8

OPTIMUM ALLOCATION OF FOREIGN EXCHANGE AMONG DIFFERENT SECTORS

8.1. NONSHIFTABILITY OF CAPITAL

In all the preceding chapters (except Chapter 5), as in most neoclassical growth models, it is assumed that capital is freely shiftable between sectors. Capital installed in one sector can be costlessly taken out of that sector and used in another sector in response to changes in profitability. Let us now depart from this unrealistic assumption and go to the other extreme of assuming complete nonshiftability of capital, that is, capital, once installed in a sector, cannot be used in any other. There is choice of sectoral allocation only at the margin of new investment decisions, but old capital goods irrevocably belong to a particular sector. This irreversibility of investment implies that different policies of sectoral allocation of current resources will give rise to different time profiles of consumption. This aspect has been emphasized in the two-sector growth models of Fel'dman [35], Domar [31], and Mohalanobis [68]. Intertemporally optimal investment allocation in such two-sector growth models has been analyzed by Johansen [48], Bose [21], and others.

A related question often arises concerning the best way of allocating a given amount of foreign exchange (received as foreign aid or earned through exports) among different sectors so as to optimize the social objective function over time. In a discussion on Indian planning, Mohalanobis [69] introduced the problem of deciding whether to use the given amount of foreign exchange to import food, or to import fertilizers, or to import fertilizer-making machines, or to import machinery for making fertilizer-making machinery. Raj and Sen [77] considered a four-sector model and calculated the rates of growth of consumption for four alternative ways of spending a given amount of foreign exchange. In comparative studies of Chinese and Indian planning it has sometimes been pointed out that Chinese planners have allocated a far larger proportion of investment and foreign exchange to machine-building, and from the long-run point of view this is sometimes regarded as a better policy (see, for example, Raj [76]). This chapter is meant to provide a simple theoretical framework for discussing this kind of issue.

We have a simple growth model with three sectors. One sector produces consumer goods (say, food grains), one produces capital goods (say, tractors) directly for the consumer goods sector, and the third represents capital goods (say, machine tools) required for further production of capital goods; the last-mentioned two sectors may be regarded as sub-branches of the "department" of capital goods in the original Marxian scheme of reproduction.[1] As in the production models of Fel'dman, Domar, and Mohalanobis, we abstract from labor as a primary factor of production for simplification. We shall try to analyze the intertemporally optimal pattern of allocation of foreign exchange in this simple growth model.

Our aim is to maximize over a finite horizon T the following social objective function:

$$\int_0^T C(t)e^{-\rho t}\, dt + K_c(T)e^{-\rho T} \qquad (1)$$

where C is consumption, K_c is the amount of tractors and ρ is the given social rate of time discount. It might possibly have been better

[1] This subclassification of the Marxian "departments" and particularly the strategic role of the machine tools sector in development planning have been emphasized by Dobb [30], Chapter IV, Raj [76], and others.

if the "scrap value" of all types of capital at the end of the planning horizon were included in the maximand along with the utility functional, but in view of the relatively complicated structure of capital in the model we find it more convenient to include only the terminal capacity in the consumer goods sector. This is undoubtedly a drastic simplification and our subsequent results on allocation of foreign exchange are obviously sensitive to this assumption (as we emphasize, for example in footnote 4). But our purpose is not to suggest realistic policy prescriptions but to provide an analytic example of an *approach* to what we regard as an important allocational problem. For the similar reason of convenience we use a linear utility function instead of our usual concave utility function. In the Appendix to this chapter we give some results for the case in which there is an infinite horizon (which does away with the arbitariness of a fixed planning horizon at the expense of some extra boundedness condition) and a concave utility function where marginal utility is diminishing.

8.2. OPTIMUM ALLOCATION OF FOREIGN EXCHANGE WITH NO DOMESTIC PRODUCTION OF MACHINE TOOLS

We are abstracting from labor as a factor of production, as we have already mentioned, and we keep a constant capital-output ratio in each sector. β_i is the output-capital ratio in the ith sector, K_i is the capital stock in the ith sector, and α_i is the proportion of foreign exchange spent in importing the ith-type good. Let us start with the case in which a constant amount of foreign exchange F is acquired each year through foreign aid (gift); we shall later take the case of foreign exchange earned through exports. We assume that ours is a small country which takes the world prices as given (assumed to be unity, without further loss of generality).

Our consumption is thus given by:

$$C(t) = \beta_c K_c(t) + \alpha_c(t)F. \tag{2}$$

The rate of accumulation of K_c (tractors) is given by:

$$\dot{K}_c(t) = \beta_I K_I(t) + \alpha_I(t)F. \tag{3}$$

For the time being let us assume that there is no domestic production of K_I, machine tools that produce tractors, and import is the only source of obtaining them. (In Section 7.3 we introduce machine tool production at home.) Thus,[2]

$$\dot{K}_I(t) = \alpha_m(t)F. \tag{4}$$

Since the α_i's are proportions,

$$\alpha_c + \alpha_I + \alpha_m = 1. \tag{5}$$

Initial stocks of capital, $K_c(0)$ and $K_I(0)$ are given. The Hamiltonian H of the present problem is given by

$$\begin{aligned} He^{\rho t} = {} & [\beta_c K_c(t) + \alpha_c(t)F] + q_c(t)[\beta_I K_I(t) + \alpha_I(t)F] \\ & + q_I(t)[1 - \alpha_c(t) - \alpha_I(t)]F, \end{aligned} \tag{6}$$

where q_c and q_I are the imputed prices of investment, $\dot{K}_c$ and $\dot{K}_I$, respectively.

The optimality conditions are given as follows:

$$\alpha_I(t)\begin{cases} = 0 & \text{if } q_c(t) < q_I(t) \\ \varepsilon[0, 1 - \alpha_c(t)] & \text{if } q_c(t) = q_I(t) \\ = 1 - \alpha_c(t) & \text{if } q_c(t) > q_I(t) \end{cases} \tag{7}$$

$$\alpha_c(t)\begin{cases} = 0 & \text{if } \max[q_c(t), q_I(t)] > 1 \\ \varepsilon[0, 1] & \text{if } \max[q_c(t), q_I(t)] = 1 \\ = 1 & \text{if } \max[q_c(t), q_I(t)] < 1. \end{cases} \tag{8}$$

In economic terms this means that we should allocate foreign exchange to the sector with the highest social demand price for a unit of foreign exchange.

$q_i(t)$ are continuous, satisfying the following:

$$\dot{q}_c(t) = \rho q_c(t) - \beta_c \tag{9}$$

$$\dot{q}_I(t) = \rho q_I(t) - \beta_I q_c(t) \tag{10}$$

$$q_c(T) = 1 \tag{11}$$

and

$$q_I(T) = 0 \tag{12}$$

[2] We are ignoring depreciation of all types of capital. A proportional rate of depreciation is not difficult to introduce in this model.

Now from (9) through (12)[3]

$$q_c(t) = \frac{\beta_c}{\rho} - e^{-\rho(T-t)}\frac{(\beta_c - \rho)}{\rho} \tag{13}$$

$$q_I(t) = \frac{\beta_I}{\rho}\left[\frac{\beta_c}{\rho}\{1 - e^{-\rho(T-t)}\} - (\beta_c - \rho)(T - t)e^{-\rho(T-t)}\right]. \tag{14}$$

In this chapter we shall assume that $\beta_i > \rho$, that is, society is not too impatient to exploit the productivity of capital in any sector.

From (11) and (13) we can immediately see that $q_c(t)$ is always greater than unity for $t < T$, so that $\max[q_c(t), q_I(t)] > 1$. From (8), this means $\alpha_c = 0$, that is, *on the optimum path we do not spend any part of foreign exchange on consumer goods.*[4] Essentially the argument is as follows: given our specific scrap-value function, with a unit increase in terminal capacity in consumer goods sector, there is a unit increase in the scrap-value function which implies that the shadow price of investing (a unit of foreign exchange) in capacity in the consumer goods sector is always larger than unity, and with a linear utility function (implying unit marginal utility) it is therefore larger than the social demand price for using a unit of foreign exchange in direct consumption. So on the optimum path in our particular model it does not pay to import consumer goods.

[3] An intuitively more obvious way of deriving (13) and (14) may be as follows. The present value of a unit of capital for consumer goods at time t is the discounted consumption stream plus its value at time t, that is,

$$e^{-\rho t}q_c(t) = \int_t^T \beta_c e^{-\rho t}\, dt + e^{-\rho t},$$

which leads to (13). Similarly the present value of a unit of tractor-making machine tools at time t is the present value of the tractor stream, that is,

$$e^{-\rho t}q_I(t) = \int_t^T \beta_I q_c(t) e^{-\rho t}\, dt,$$

which leads to (14).

[4] This result will change if we do not include $K_c(T)$ in the objective function along with the utility functional. If no terminal capacity constraints are assumed, then $q_c(T) = q_I(T) = 0$. In this case we shall have a terminal phase on the optimum path when we import consumer goods. On the other hand if we have a scrap value function which is $[K_c(T) + K_I(T)]e^{-\rho T}$, then once again on the optimum path $\alpha_c = 0$; but in this case the sign of (15) would depend on the comparison of β_I and β_c.

From (13) and (14),

$$q_I(T-t) - q_c(T-t) = \frac{e^{-\rho t}}{\rho^2}\,[(e^{\rho t}-1)\,\beta_c(\beta_I-\rho) - \beta_I(\beta_c-\rho)\rho t - \rho^2]. \tag{15}$$

If we call the bracketed expression on the right-hand side of (15) $f(x)$, where $x = \rho t$, then it is easy to see that there exists a unique positive x^* such that $f(x^*) = 0$. This is shown in Figure 8.1. It is

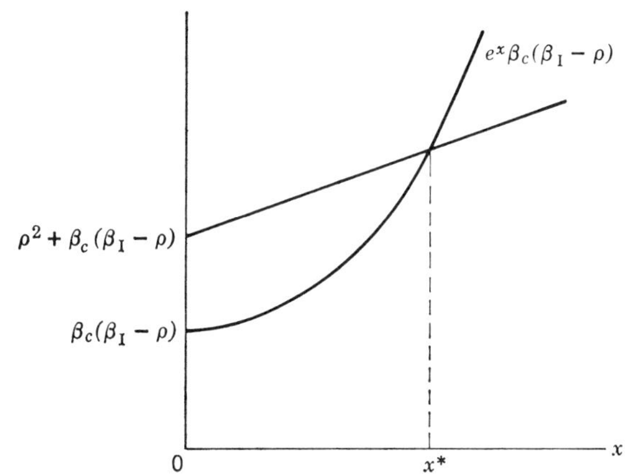

Figure 8.1

also easy to establish that $f'(x^*) > 0$. All this means that there exists a unique positive τ such that

$$q_I(T-t) - q_c(T-t) \gtreqless 0 \qquad \text{as } t \gtreqless \tau. \tag{16}$$

Figure 8.2 depicts this.

From (7) we may now say that *on the optimum path, in the first phase (up to time $T-\tau$) we spend all of our foreign exchange F in importing machine tools* ($\alpha_m = 1$, $\alpha\ = \alpha_c = 0$), *and in the second phase we spend all of it in importing tractors* ($\alpha_I = 1$, $\alpha_m = \alpha_c = 0$). It is also important to note that τ is independent of T, so that the time spent on the optimum path when all foreign exchange is used to buy tractors is the same irrespective of the planning horizon and *the longer the horizon the larger the proportion of time on the optimum path when all foreign exchange is spent on importing machine tools.*

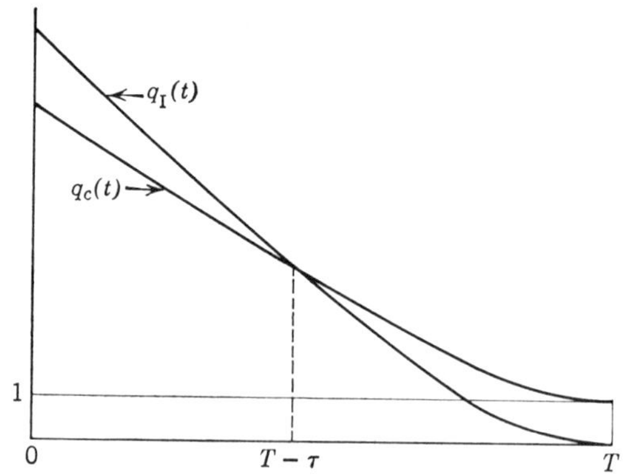

Figure 8.2

In the Appendix to this chapter we consider the same allocation problem but with a planning horizon that is infinite and with a nonlinear instantaneous utility function. We have not been able to completely characterize the optimum path but on the basis of our calculations in the Appendix, we can report here that $\alpha_c(t) = \alpha_I(t) = 0$ and $\alpha_m(t) = 1$ is the *asymptotically* optimal policy, that is, "in the long run" we should spend *all* of our foreign exchange in importing machine tools. This ties up with our finding in the finite-horizon case that the longer the planning horizon the larger the proportion of time spent in importing only machine tools.

8.3. OPTIMUM ALLOCATION WITH DOMESTIC PRODUCTION OF MACHINE TOOLS

In this section we go back to the finite-horizon case but make the model more complicated by introducing domestic production of machine tools. These machine tools may be used to produce either tractors or more machine tools, and the allocation of the machine tools between the two uses has now to be decided, apart from the sectoral allocation of foreign exchange, on the basis of the optimization process.

Equation (4) in Section 8.2 must now be rewritten as

$$\dot{K}_I(t) + \dot{K}_m(t) = \beta_m K_m(t) + \alpha_m(t)F \tag{17}$$

$$\dot{K}_I = \lambda(t)[\dot{K}_I + \dot{K}_m], \tag{18}$$

where λ is the proportion of the amount of machine tools currently available to be used in the production of tractors,

$$1 \geq \lambda(t) \geq 0. \tag{19}$$

The Hamiltonian H of (6) now must be rewritten as

$$\begin{aligned} He^{\rho t} = [\beta_c K_c(t) + \alpha_c(t)F] + q_c(t)[\beta_I K_I(t) + \alpha_I(t)F] \\ + q(t)[\beta_m K_m(t) + \{1 - \alpha_c(t) - \alpha_I(t)\}F], \end{aligned} \tag{20}$$

where $q(t) = \lambda(t)q_I(t) + [1 - \lambda(t)]q_m(t)$ and $q_m(t)$ is the imputed price of investment in the machine tools sector.

The optimality conditions are as follows:

$$\lambda(t)\begin{cases} = 0 & \text{if } q_I(t) < q_m(t) \\ \varepsilon[0, 1] & \text{if } q_I(t) = q_m(t) \\ = 1 & \text{if } q_I(t) > q_m(t), \end{cases} \tag{21}$$

so that

$$q(t) = \max[q_I(t), q_m(t)], \tag{22}$$

$$\alpha_I(t)\begin{cases} = 0 & \text{if } q_c(t) < q(t) \\ \varepsilon[0, 1 - \alpha_c(t)] & \text{if } q_c(t) = q(t) \\ = 1 - \alpha_c(t) & \text{if } q_c(t) > q(t) \end{cases} \tag{23}$$

$$\alpha_c(t)\begin{cases} = 0 & \text{if } \max[q_c(t), q(t)] > 1 \\ \varepsilon[0, 1] & \text{if } \max[q_c(t), q(t)] = 1 \\ = 1 & \text{if } \max[q_c(t), q(t)] < 1, \end{cases} \tag{24}$$

$q_i(t)$ are continuous, satisfying (9), (10), (11), and

$$\dot{q}_m(t) = \rho q_m(t) - \beta_m q(t) \tag{25}$$

$$q_I(T) = q_m(T) = 0. \tag{26}$$

Now $q_c(t)$ and $q_I(t)$ are given, as before, by (13) and (14). We first solve for $q_m(t)$, *assuming* $q(t) = q_I(t)$ and using (25) and (26). This gives,

$$\begin{aligned} q_m(t) = e^{-\rho(T-t)} \frac{\beta_I \beta_m}{\rho^2} \Bigg[\frac{\beta_c}{\rho} \{e^{\rho(T-t)} - 1\} \\ - \left\{(\beta_c - \rho)\rho\left(\frac{T^2}{2} - tT + \frac{t^2}{2}\right) + \beta_c(T - t)\right\}\Bigg]. \end{aligned} \tag{27}$$

From (14) and (27),

$$q_I(T-t) - q_m(T-t) = \left[\frac{\beta_m}{2}(\beta_c - \rho)x + \rho^2 + \beta_c(\beta_m - \rho) - \frac{(e^x - 1)}{x}\beta_c(\beta_m - \rho)\right] xe^{-x}\frac{\beta_I}{\rho^3}, \tag{28}$$

where $x = \rho t$.

If we call the bracketed expression on the right-hand side of (28) $g(x)$, then it is easy to see that there exists a unique positive x^{**} such that $g(x^{**}) = 0$. This is shown in Figure 8.3. It is also easy to

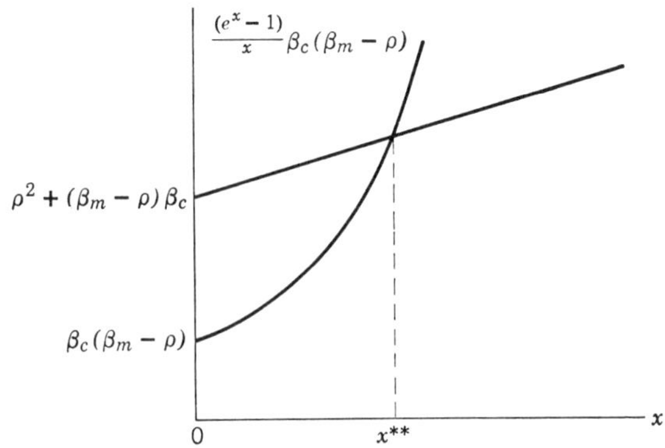

Figure 8.3

see that $g'(x^{**}) < 0$. All this means that there exists a unique positive t^* such that

$$q_I(T-t) - q_m(T-t) \gtreqless 0 \qquad \text{as} \qquad t \lesseqgtr t^*. \tag{29}$$

Figure 8.4 depicts this. From (21) we may now say that *on the optimum path from the beginning up to time $T - t^*$ all of the flow of machine tools currently available is used in producing more machine tools (that is, $\lambda = 0$) and, after that, all of it is used in producing tractors (that is, $\lambda = 1$)*. Let us call the first phase A (when $\lambda = 0$), and the second phase B (when $\lambda = 1$). We have yet to find out the pattern of α_i's (indicating the allocation of foreign exchange) in these two phases.

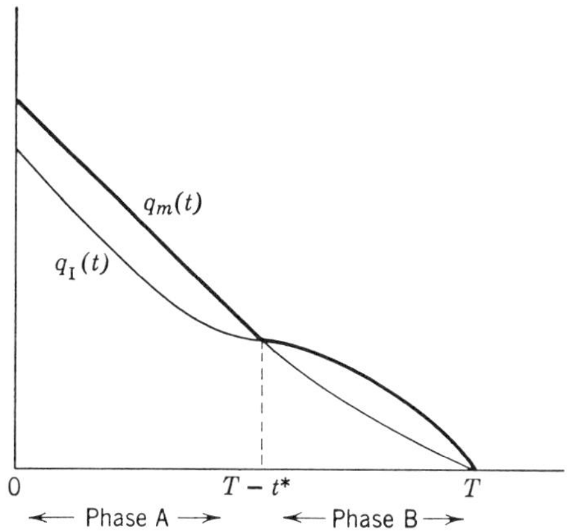

Figure 8.4

As in Section 8.2, $q_c(t)$ is always greater than unity until $q_c(T) = 1$. From (24) this means, once again, that α_c is always zero, that is, *on the optimum path we spend no part of our foreign exchange in importing consumer goods.*

For determining the pattern of $\alpha_I(t)$ we have to compare $q_c(t)$ with $q(t)$. From (22) we know that the path of $q(t)$ is depicted by the heavy line in Figure 8.4. Both $q(t)$ and $q_c(t)$ are declining functions of time.

From (9) (10), and (25) it is obvious that the $q(t)$ and $q_c(t)$ curves cannot cross more than once in either phase A or phase B. In fact, one can prove a stronger result. In both the phases taken together there cannot be more than one crossing of the $q(t)$ and $q_c(t)$ curves. Let us give a short proof of the latter proposition.

Suppose $q(t)$ and $q_c(t)$ curves cross twice, once at time $T - \tau'$ $(t^* < \tau')$ and again at time $T - \tau$ $(t^* > \tau)$, so that $q_c(T - \tau') = q(T - \tau') = q_m(T - \tau')$ and $q_c(T - \tau) = q(T - \tau) = q_I(T - \tau)$. With $q_c(T) = 1$ and $q(T) = 0$, this implies that

$$\dot{q}_c(T - \tau) > \dot{q}_I(T - \tau) \tag{30}$$

and

$$\dot{q}_c(T - \tau') < \dot{q}_m(T - \tau'). \tag{31}$$

From (9) and (10), (30) implies

$$q_c(T - \tau) + q_I(T - \tau) > \frac{\beta_c}{\beta_I}. \tag{32}$$

From (9) and (25), (31) implies

$$\frac{\beta_c}{\beta_m} > q_c(T - \tau') = q_m(T - \tau'). \tag{33}$$

We know from (29) that

$$q_I(T - t^*) = q_m(T - t^*)$$

and

$$\dot{q}_I(T - t^*) > \dot{q}_m(T - t^*).$$

From (10) and (25) this means that

$$q_m(T - t^*) = q_I(T - t^*) > \frac{\beta_I}{\beta_m} q_c(T - t^*). \tag{34}$$

Now if we put (32), (33), and (34) together,

$$\frac{\beta_c}{\beta_m} > q_m(T - \tau') > q_m(T - t^*) > \frac{\beta_I}{\beta_m} q_c(T - t^*) > \frac{\beta_I}{\beta_m} q_c(T - \tau) > \frac{\beta_c}{\beta_m},$$

which is a contradiction. This means that $q(t)$ and $q_c(t)$ curves can never cross more than once. In other words, there is no "reswitching."

Let us now prove that if $\beta_I \geq \beta_m$, the $q_c(t)$ curve *must* cross the $q(t)$ curve in what we have called Phase B, as in Figure 8.5. If the

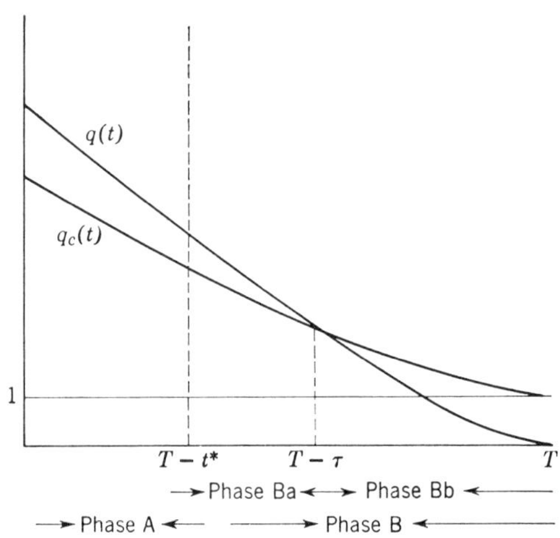

Figure 8.5

$q_c(t)$ curve does *not* cross the $q(t)$ curve in Phase B, since $q_c(T) = 1$ and since in phase B $q(t) = q_I(t)$, this means

$$q_c(T - t^*) > q_I(T - t^*)$$

If $\beta_I \geq \beta_m$ this is in contradiction to (34).

So in Figure 8.5 Phase B is in two subphases, Phase Ba ($T - \tau > t > T - t^*$) when $q(t) > q_c(t)$ and hence $\alpha_I = 0$ along with $\lambda - 1$, and Phase Bb ($T > t > T - \tau$) when $q_c(t) > q(t)$ and hence $\alpha_I = 1$ along with $\lambda = 1$. Since the $q_c(t)$ and $q(t)$ curves can cross only once, in Phase A the $q(t)$ curve lies always about the $q_c(t)$ curve and $\alpha_I = 0$ along with $\lambda = 0$.

What if $\beta_m > \beta_I$? In this case we are not so sure. We know, of course, that the $q_c(t)$ and $q(t)$ curves can cross once *at most*. We can go somewhat beyond and say that if the planning horizon T is sufficiently large, there must be one crossing. This is because the expression for $[q_m(0) - q_c(0)]$ is positive for T large, and with $q_m(0) > q_c(0)$ there must be a crossing of $q_c(t)$ and $q(t)$, either in Phase A or in Phase B. So for large T the $q_c(t)$ curve cannot always lie above the $q(t)$ curve to make α_I always equal to unity.

In the summary of this section, if $\beta_I \geq \beta_m$, that is, if the output-capital ratio in the tractors sector is not less than that in the machine tools sector, or roughly speaking, *if machine tools are not less capital-intensive than tractors, the optimum path has three uniquely determined phases: the first phase when we spend all of our foreign exchange in importing machine tools and devote all of our currently available flow of machine tools to the production of more machine tools*; *the second phase when we spend all of our foreign exchange in importing machine tools but use all machine tools for producing tractors; and the third phase when we spend all of our foreign exchange in importing tractors and use all of the current output of machine tools for producing tractors.* The length of the last two phases is independent of T, the planning horizon, and the longer the horizon the more the first phase predominates.

When machine tools are less capital-intensive than tractors, then there are also two distinct phases, one phase in which all machine tools are used for producing more machine tools, followed by the next phase in which all machine tools are used for producing tractors. Again, the longer the planning horizon, the more the first phase will predominate. Regarding the allocation of foreign exchange there is less certainty, but either we spend all of our foreign exchange in importing tractors or, if the planning horizon is long enough, we spend all of our foreign exchange first in importing machine tools and then spend all of it in importing tractors; in no case is there importation of consumer goods and in no case is there subsequent reswitching to an earlier allocation policy.

We have so far assumed that ours is a small country which takes world prices as given and receives at each point in time a constant amount of foreign exchange through foreign aid. Let us now change the model and assume that we *earn* this foreign exchange through exports of our consumer goods, which we shall call X_c. Suppose we are an important exporter of these consumer goods and can therefore affect their world price P_c, but when we buy imports (tractors and machine tools) we are not big enough buyers in the world market to affect their prices so that they are again taken as given. As we have commented in section 6.2, this is not an unfamiliar situation for many developing countries.

For simplification we take a specific world demand function for our exports of consumer goods:

$$X_c(t) = P_c^{\eta}(t) \quad \text{with} \quad \eta < 0, 1 + \eta < 0,$$

where η is the constant price elasticity of demand, the absolute value of which is assumed to be greater than unity. So our earning of foreign exchange at time t is now given by our export receipts

$$P_c(t)X_c(t) = X_c^{(1+\eta)/\eta}(t). \tag{35}$$

The Hamiltonian H in (21) now must be rewritten as

$$\begin{aligned} He^{\rho t} = [\beta_c K_c(t) - X_c(t)] + q_c(t)[\beta_I K_I(t) + \alpha_I(t) X_c^{1+\eta/\eta}(t)] \\ + q(t)[\beta_m K_m(t) + \{1 - \alpha_I(t)\} X_c^{(1+\eta)/\eta}(t)]. \end{aligned} \tag{36}$$

We assume positive consumption and positive exports so that

$$\beta_c K_c(t) > X_c(t) > 0.$$

If we now maximize the Hamiltonian with respect to $\alpha_I(t)$, $\lambda(t)$, and $X_c(t)$, we obtain (21), (22), and (23), as before (with $\alpha_c = 0$), and the extra condition

$$[\alpha_I(t) q_c(t) + \{1 - \alpha_I(t)\} q(t)] = \frac{\eta}{1+\eta} X_c^{-1/\eta}(t). \tag{37}$$

Equations (9), (10), (11), (25), and (26) will also stand as before.

So the analysis of the behavior of the $q_c(t)$, $q_I(t)$, and $q_m(t)$ curves—and hence the behavior of $\alpha_I(t)$, $\alpha_m(t)$, and $\lambda(t)$—is exactly the same. The only new condition is (37), which implies that we should choose the quantity of our exports in such a way that the *marginal* terms of trade (which are less than the average terms of trade), $P_c(t)[1 + \eta]/\eta$, are equal to the reciprocal of $\bar{q}(t)$, where $\bar{q}(t) = \max[q_c(t), q(t)]$. Since both $q_c(t)$ and $q(t)$ are declining functions of time, it is easy to see that on the optimum path we export less and less over time and retain more for consumption.

Going back to the case when we have no exports but obtain a constant amount of foreign exchange through foreign aid, in the Appendix we consider the same allocation problem as in this section, but the planning horizon is infinite and the maximand is a discounted (strictly) concave utility functional. This seems to be a fairly difficult problem [in the sense that it is hard to keep track of all the possible switchings of the $q_i(t)$ curves]. All we can report here on the basis of our calculations in the Appendix is as follows: (a) In the terminal phase of the optimal trajectory the available flow of machine tools is used in producing *both* tractors and machine tools (that is, $1 > \lambda > 0$). (b) In the terminal phase of the optimal path we spend *all* of our foreign exchange in importing machine tools if $\beta_I > \beta_m$ *and* $\beta_c \geq \beta_m$, or *all* of it in importing tractors if $\beta_m > \beta_I$ *and* $\beta_m > \beta_c$, or *all* of it in importing consumer goods if $\beta_m > \beta_I$ *and* $\beta_c > \beta_m$.

There are at least two important ways the model in this chapter should be extended, although we have not done it here. One is to introduce intermediate products that are produced and imported and are used in other sectors. The other is to introduce labor as a primary factor of production.[5] Both of these will make the analysis of our present problem much more complicated. One can be sure, however, that the introduction of a second factor of production (such as labor) with diminishing marginal productivity of factors will add sufficient concavity to the maximand to do away with the extreme "bang-bang" type allocation policy described in much of this chapter.

Quite often a rough justification for not using labor as a factor of

[5] For an analysis of optimum growth in a two-sector, closed-economy, non-shiftable capital model with labor as a shiftable primary factor of production, see Bose [22].

production in simple development planning models is cited in terms of the "surplus labor" hypothesis for many overpopulated developing economies. Even if one overlooks the empirical doubts about this hypothesis, it ignores the institutional factors under which any transfer of labor from the food grains-producing sector to the machine-producing sector raises the problem of obtaining enough grains to feed the additional laborers. (This problem is analyzed in the context of an open economy in Chapter 9.) From the standpoint of development planning under the typical institutional constraints food is a kind of capital good (this is in some sense akin to the concept of wages-fund or circulating capital of the classical economists) and in a more complete model of optimum foreign exchange allocation than the one studied in this chapter, this increases the importance of spending foreign exchange on food.

APPENDIX: INFINITE HORIZON

Suppose the social objective is to maximize the integral of a constant-elasticity instantaneous utility function over an infinite horizon:

$$\max \int_0^{\infty} \frac{C(t)^{1-\theta}}{1-\theta} e^{-\rho t}\, dt.$$

Subject to (2), (3), (4), and (5), where θ is the absolute value of the elasticity of marginal utility.

The necessary conditions for optimality are given by (7), (10), (38), and (39):

$$\alpha_c(t) \begin{cases} = 0 & \text{if } \max[q_c(t), q_I(t)] > C(t)^{-\theta} \\ \varepsilon[0, 1] & \text{if } \max[q_c(t), q_I(t)] = C(t)^{-\theta} \\ = 1 & \text{if } \max[q_c(t), q_I(t)] < C(t)^{-\theta} \end{cases} \tag{38}$$

$$\dot{q}_c(t) = \rho q_c(t) - \beta_c C(t)^{-\theta}. \tag{39}$$

Since the utility function is concave, the following transversality conditions are sufficient for optimality:

$$\lim_{t\to\infty} q_i(t)e^{-\rho t}K_i(t) = 0; \qquad \lim_{t\to\infty} q_i(t) \geq 0, \qquad i = c, I. \tag{40}$$

We shall prove here that the *asymptotically optimal* policy in this case is to spend *all* of foreign exchange in importing machine tools (that is, $\alpha_m = 1$, $\alpha_c = \alpha_I = 0$).

From (39) and (10),

$$q_c(t) = e^{\rho t}\left[q_c(0) - \beta_c \int_0^t e^{-\rho v}\psi(v)\,dv\right] \tag{41}$$

$$q_I(t) = e^{\rho t}\left[q_I(0) - \beta_I \int_0^t e^{-\rho v}q_c(v)\,dv\right], \tag{42}$$

where

$$\psi(t) \equiv \overset{-\theta}{C(t)}.$$

Since $K_c(t)$ and $K_I(t)$ are increasing functions of time, the transversality conditions (40) imply that

$$q_c(0) = \beta_c \int_0^\infty e^{-\rho v}\psi(v)\,dv \tag{43}$$

and

$$q_I(0) = \beta_I \int_0^\infty e^{-\rho v}q_c(v)\,dv. \tag{44}$$

Using (43) and (44) in (41) and (42),

$$q_c(t) = e^{\rho t}\beta_c \int_t^\infty e^{-\rho v}\psi(v)\,dv \tag{45}$$

$$q_I(t) = e^{\rho t}\beta_I \int_t^\infty e^{-\rho v}q_c(v)\,dv. \tag{46}$$

We shall now prove that $q_I(t) > q_c(t)$ and $q_I(t) > \psi(t)$ as $t \to \infty$.

From (45) and (46),

$$q_I(t) - q_c(t) = e^{\rho t}\int_t^\infty e^{-\rho v}[\beta_I q_c(v) - \beta_c \psi(v)]\,dv. \tag{47}$$

Calling $V(t) = \beta_I q_c(t) - \beta_c \psi(t)$, then from (45),

$$V(t) = \beta_I e^{\rho t} \beta_c \int_t^\infty e^{-\rho v} \psi(v)\, dv - \beta_c \psi(t)$$

$$= \frac{\beta_I}{\rho} e^{\rho t} \beta_c \left[e^{-\rho t} \psi(t) + \int_t^\infty e^{-\rho v} \psi'(v)\, dv - \lim_{t \to \infty} e^{-\rho v} \psi(v) \right]$$

$$- \beta_c \psi(t),$$

through integration by parts. Thus,

$$V(t) = \beta_c \psi(t) \frac{(\beta_I - \rho)}{\rho} + \frac{\beta_I \beta_c}{\rho} e^{\rho t} \int_t^\infty e^{-\rho v} \psi'(v)\, dv,$$

since

$$\lim_{v \to \infty} e^{-\rho v} \psi(v) = 0.$$

Therefore $V(t) > 0$, if

$$\frac{(\beta_I - \rho)}{\beta_I} > \frac{-\int_t^\infty e^{-\rho v} \psi'(v)\, dv}{\psi(t) e^{-\rho t}}. \tag{48}$$

Let us call the right-hand side of (48) $f(t)/g(t)$. We know that $f(\infty) = 0$ and $g(\infty) = 0$. So,

$$\lim_{t \to \infty} \frac{f(t)}{\mu(t)} = \lim_{t \to \infty} \frac{f'(t)}{g'(t)} = \lim_{t \to \infty} \frac{1}{\left[1 - \rho \dfrac{\psi(t)}{\psi'(t)}\right]} = \lim_{t \to \infty} \frac{1}{\left[1 + \dfrac{\rho K_c(t)}{\theta \dot{K}_c(t)}\right]} = 0,$$

since

$$\psi(t) = \overset{-\theta}{C(t)}, \qquad C(t) = \beta_c K_c(t),$$

α_i's are bounded from above and with the use of L'Hospital's rule $\dot{K}_c(t)/K_c(t) \to 0$ as $t \to \infty$.

So from (48), as $t \to \infty$, $V(t) > 0$ and hence (47) is positive. Now from (46),

$$q_I(t) - \psi(t) = e^{\rho t} \beta_I \int_t^\infty e^{-\rho v} q_c(v)\, dv - \psi(t)$$

$$= e^{\rho t} \beta_I \int_t^\infty \int_v^\infty e^{-\rho \tau} \beta_c \psi(\tau)\, d\tau\, dv - \psi(t)$$

$$= e^{\rho t} \frac{\beta_I \beta_c}{\rho} \int_t^\infty e^{-\rho v} \psi(v)[1 - X(v)]\, dv - \psi(t), \tag{49}$$

where

$$X(v) = \frac{-\int_v^\infty e^{-\rho\tau}\psi'(\tau)\,d\tau}{e^{-\rho v}\psi(v)}.$$

We have already proved that $X(v) \to 0$, as $v \to \infty$. Equation (49) will be positive if we can prove that as $t \to \infty$

$$\frac{\int_t^\infty e^{-\rho v}\psi(v)[1 - X(v)]\,dv}{e^{-\rho t}\psi(t)} > \frac{\rho}{\beta_I \beta_c}. \tag{50}$$

Let us call the right-hand side of (50) $s(t)/p(t)$.
We know that $s(\infty) = 0$ and $p(\infty) = 0$. So,

$$\lim_{t\to\infty} \frac{s(t)}{p(t)} = \lim_{t\to\infty} \frac{s'(t)}{p'(t)} - \lim_{t\to\infty} \frac{[1 - X(t)]}{\left[\rho - \dfrac{\psi'(t)}{\psi(t)}\right]} = \lim_{t\to\infty} \frac{[1 - X(t)\}}{\left[\rho + \theta \dfrac{\dot{K}_c(t)}{K_c(t)}\right]} = \frac{1}{\rho}. \tag{51}$$

Since $\beta_I > \rho$, $\beta_c > \rho$, (51) implies the validity of (50). Thus, we have proved that as $t \to \infty$, $q_I(t) > q_c(t)$ and $q_I(t) > \psi(t)$ and hence $\alpha_c = \alpha_I = 0$ and $\alpha_m = 1$ *is* the asymptotically optimal policy.

Let us now take the allocation problem of Section 8.3 when we have domestic production of machine tools, but introduce an infinite horizon and a nonlinear instantaneous utility function of the form

$$U(c) = \frac{C(t)^{-\theta}}{1 - \theta}.$$

Let us maximize the utility functional subject to (2), (3), (5), (17), (18), and (19). The necessary conditions for optimality are given by (21), (22), (23), (38), (10), (25), and (39). The transversality conditions are given by (40). Now if the system remains in the phase when $1 > \lambda(t) > 0$ for an interval $[t_0, t_1]$, then for $t_1 > t > t_0$:

$$q_I(t) = q_m(t) = q^*(t). \tag{52}$$

Using (39), (10), and (25), (52) implies that

$$q^*(t) = \frac{\beta_I}{\beta_m} q_c(t) = \frac{\beta_I \beta_c}{\beta_m^2} \psi(t). \tag{53}$$

Using (22) and (38), (53) means that for $t_1 > t > t_0$, if $\beta_I > \beta_m$ and $\beta_c \geq \beta_m$, then $q^*(t) > q_c(t)$ and $q^*(t) \gtrless \psi(t)$, so that

$$\alpha_I = \alpha_c = 0 \qquad \text{and} \qquad \alpha_m = 1; \tag{54}$$

if $\beta_m > \beta_I$ and $\beta_m > \beta_c$, then $q^*(t) < q_c(t)$ and $q_c(t) > \psi(t)$, so that

$$\alpha_c = \alpha_m = 0 \qquad \text{and} \qquad \alpha_I = 1; \tag{55}$$

and if $\beta_m > \beta_I$ and $\beta_c > \beta_m$, then $q^*(t) < q_c(t)$ and $q_c(t) < \psi(t)$, so that

$$\alpha_I = \alpha_m = 0 \qquad \text{and} \qquad \alpha_c = 1. \tag{56}$$

Let us first take the case in which the sectoral capital intensities are such that (54) is valid. In this case

$$K_c(t) = K_c(t_0) e^{[(\beta_m - \rho)/\theta](t - t_0)} \tag{57}$$

$$K_I(t) = \frac{(\beta_m - \rho)}{\theta \beta_I} K_c(t) \tag{58}$$

and

$$K_m(t) = \left[K_m(t_0) + \frac{F}{\beta_m} - \frac{K_c(t_0)(\beta_m - \rho)^2}{\theta \beta_I \{\rho - \beta_m(1 - \theta)\}} \right] e^{\beta_m (t - t_0)} - \frac{F}{\beta_m} + \frac{K_c(t)(\beta_m - \rho)^2}{\theta \beta_I \{\rho - \beta_m(1 - \theta)\}}. \tag{59}$$

We assume that $\{\rho - \beta_m(1 - \theta)\}$ is positive, which is a boundedness assumption on the maximand integral of the problem. From (53), (57), (58), and (59) it follows that

$$\lim_{t \to \infty} e^{-\rho t} q_c(t) K_c(t) = \lim_{t \to \infty} \frac{\{\beta_c K_c(t_0)\}^{1-\theta}}{\beta_m} e^{-\{\rho - (1-\theta)\beta_m\}} \frac{(t - t_0)}{\theta} = 0 \tag{60}$$

$$\lim_{t \to \infty} e^{-\rho t} q_I(t) K_I(t) = \lim_{t \to \infty} \frac{\beta_c^{1-\theta} (\beta_m - \rho) K_c^{1-\theta}(t_0)}{\beta_m^2 \theta} \times e^{-\{\rho - (1-\theta)\beta_m\}} \frac{(t - t_0)}{\theta} = 0, \tag{61}$$

but

$$\lim_{t \to \infty} e^{-\rho t} q_m(t) K_m(t) = 0,$$

only if

$$K_m(t_0) + \frac{F}{\beta_m} = \frac{K_c(t_0)(\beta_m - \rho)^2}{\theta \beta_I \{\rho - \beta_m(1 - \theta)\}}, \tag{62}$$

so that

$$K_m(t) = \frac{K_c(t)(\beta_m - \rho)^2}{\theta^2 \beta_I \{\rho - \beta_m(1 - \theta)\}} - \frac{F}{\beta_m}. \tag{63}$$

So in the phase when $1 > \lambda(t) > 0$ the only trajectory that satisfies the transversality conditions is the one characterized by solutions of $K_c(t)$, $K_I(t)$, and $K_m(t)$ as given by (57), (58), and (63). As $t \to \infty$, this path also dominates any other path with $\lambda = 0$ or $\lambda = 1$, so that this must be the terminal phase of the optimal trajectory. The proportion of currently available machine tools to be used to producing tractors on this terminal phase of the optimal trajectory, λ^*, is given by:

$$\lambda^* = \frac{\rho - \beta_m(1 - \theta)}{\theta \beta_m} \varepsilon [0, 1]. \tag{64}$$

Using similar methods, we can show that if the sectoral capital intensities are such that (55) is valid, then the transversality conditions are satisfied in the phase when $1 > \lambda(t) > 0$ only if

$$K_m(t_0) = \frac{K_c(t_0)(\beta_m - \rho)^2}{\theta \beta_I \{\rho - \beta_m(1 - \theta)\}}. \tag{65}$$

Once again this must be the terminal phase of the optimal trajectory and λ^* is the same as in (64). Similarly we can show that if the sectoral capital intensities are such that (56) is valid, then the transversality conditions are satisfied in the phase when $1 > \lambda(t) > 0$ only if

$$K_m(t_0) = \frac{(\beta_m - \rho)^2}{\theta \beta_I} \left[\frac{F}{\theta \beta_c \beta_m} + \frac{K_c(t_0)}{\{\rho - \beta_m(1 - \theta)\}} \right]. \tag{66}$$

Again, this must be the terminal phase of the optimal trajectory. In this case $\lambda^*(t)$ is given by

$$\lambda^*(t) = \frac{\beta_c K_c(t) + F}{F + \dfrac{\theta \beta_c \beta_m K_c(t)}{\{\rho - \beta_m(1-\theta)\}}} \varepsilon[0, 1]; \tag{67}$$

as $t \to \infty$,

$$\lambda^* \to \frac{\rho - \beta_m(1-\theta)}{\theta \beta_m}.$$

9

OPTIMUM TRADE POLICY IN A DUAL ECONOMY

9.1. TRADE AND THE PREOBRAZHENSKY DILEMMA

The standard aggregative models of development planning for a dual economy incorporate two important institutional assumptions: (a) the industrial sector is more or less under the direct control of the government, whereas the agricultural sector is largely in the hands of private cultivators and (b) the industrial *real* wage rate is institutionally fixed. These two typical institutional assumptions, together with a third institutional presumption that it is politically difficult to implement any program of substantial *direct* taxation of agriculture in most developing economies, make the problem of ensuring sufficient marketed surplus of food one of the most important problems of development. For rapid growth of the economy, the planner wants to ensure more production of industrial goods which include investment goods, but that involves more industrial employment and transfer of labor from the agricultural sector. Since industrial workers at their low levels of income spend most of their wages on food, the government needs more food to feed the growing industrial labor force. Under the institutional assumptions made, the government is denied both compulsory procurement (such as that in Soviet Union after agricultural collectivization) and heavy direct taxation of agriculture (such as land taxation in Meiji, Japan[1]) as significant ways of tapping the agricultural surplus. Thus, the only major ways of obtaining more food are either (a) to exert the government monopsony power[2] in buying food by suitably manipulating price policy or (b) to invest more in the production of agricultural input that help food production and therefore sales. The difficulty with (a) is that if the industrial real wage in terms of food is institutionally given, then higher food prices which might be needed to encourage more sales from farmers will raise the industrial wage bill and thus cut down on the industrial investible surplus and capital accumulation. The difficulty with (b) is that more investment in agricultural inputs will again reduce industrial capital accumulation. The essential trade-offs involved contribute to an interesting exercise in intertemporal optimization which has hardly been attempted in the literature.[3]

[1] The contribution of land taxes to mobilization of agricultural surplus in Japan after the Meiji Restoration has sometimes been overplayed in the literature. Nakamura [70] points out that high rural savings in Meiji Japan were mainly a result of drastic land reforms in the early Meiji period which redistributed income from the ruling classes (particularly the *samurai*) of the Tokugawa period to the land-owning classes who had a larger propensity to save, and that direct taxes as proportion of agricultural output were actually much lower in the Meiji period than in the preceding Tokugawa period.

[2] As early as 1926, the Soviet economist Preobrazhensky [75], p. 111, suggested in this context, among other things, the "carrying out on the basis of monopoly a price policy which will be only another form of taxation of private economy." (I am indebted to S. Bose for bringing this passage to my attention.)

Preobrazhensky seems to have been among the first economists to grapple with the marketed surplus problem and all the dilemmas that arise in rapid industrialization in a partially planned economy in which industry is largely state-owned but agriculture is run by private farms: the problems of what he called "primitive socialist accumulation" that were being faced in the Soviet Union of the 1920's. Agricultural collectivization was Stalin's solution to the Preobrazhensky dilemma in the beginning of the 1930's.

[3] Some partial attempts have been made by Findlay [36], and very recently by Hornby [47] and Bose and Dixit [23]. More attention in the literature on dual-economy planning has been concentrated on the intertemporal optimization problem involved in choosing the right techniques of industrial production because of the link between capital intensity of techniques and savings. See

Foreign trade and borrowing enabling imports of food and agricultural inputs are partial solutions to the problems mentioned above, although more imports mean more diversion of investible resources to the export industries (even assuming that there is no external demand bottleneck limiting export possibilities), and as for borrowing, much depends on the rate of interest charged and the repayment schedule. Our purpose in this chapter is to analyze the problems of optimum development policy in the context of a simple model of such a dual economy open to foreign trade and borrowing.

The industrial sector directly controlled by the government produces two goods, good m—which is either consumable (textiles) or investible (machines)[4]—and good n which is an agricultural input (fertilizer). Their production functions are given by

$$F_i = F_i(K_i, L_i), \qquad i = m, n \tag{1}$$

where F_i is the output of the ith good, K_i and L_i are the amounts of capital and labor employed, respectively, in producing the ith good. The production functions are assumed to be of constant returns to scale.

The total industrial labor force is given by

$$L = L_m + L_n. \tag{2}$$

The industrial wage rate deflated by the domestic price of food P_f is an institutionally given constant $\overline{W}$. The total industrial wage bill is therefore given by $P_f \overline{W} L$. Since we are assuming all wages to be consumed,

$$P_f \overline{W} L = P_f C_f + C_m \tag{3}$$

where C_f is the amount of food consumed and C_m is the amount of textiles consumed by the industrial labor force. Good m is being taken as the *numéraire*. We shall assume that in the industrial sector the laborers are the only consumers and that all remaining industrial surplus is invested.

Eckstein [32], Sen [86], Marglin [62], and Dixit [29]. The historical-descriptive literature on the development of dual economy has also largely ignored the issues raised by the marketed surplus problem. See, for example, Jorgenson [53] and Ranis and Fei [79].

[4] For simplification we are assuming that textiles and machines are produced on the same production function.

Total industrial consumption of food is out of supplies from the domestic agricultural sector or imports, so that

$$C_f = S + Z_f, \tag{4}$$

where S is the surplus of food marketed by the agricultural sector and Z_f is the amount imported of food. It is being assumed that all foreign trade (and borrowing) is directly handled by the government and that all imported food is distributed only in the industrial sector.

The total amount N of fertilizers used in agricultural production comes either from domestic production of fertilizers in the industrial sector or from imports, so that

$$N = F_n + Z_n, \tag{5}$$

where Z_n is the amount of n imported.

As in Section 6.2 we assume that foreign trade is balanced not instantaneously but over the planning horizon T so that

$$\int_0^T [\bar{P}_f Z_f + \bar{P}_n Z_n + Z_m] e^{-rt}\, dt = 0, \tag{6}$$

where $\bar{P}_i$ is the fixed international price of the ith good, $(i = f, n)$, Z_m is the amount of m imported (textiles or machines), and r is the given rate of interest at which the country can borrow from abroad to cover a current deficit. We are assuming that the country is neither a big enough buyer or seller of goods in the world goods market (we shall relax this assumption later) nor a big enough borrower or lender in the world capital market to be able to affect the international prices or the rate of interest.

Vis-à-vis the domestic agricultural sector, the industrial sector faces a marketed-surplus function (offer curve) for food by cultivators, so that

$$S = S(P_f, N). \tag{7}$$

Marketed surplus is directly a function of P_f in the sense that if the government, the monopsonistic buyer of food, raises its price, more food will be sold by cultivators,[5] that is,

$$S_1 = \left(\frac{\partial S}{\partial P_f}\right)_{N \text{ constant}} > 0.$$

[5] There is a growing volume of literature on estimation of price elasticity of marketed surplus of food grains in peasant economies. It is generally agreed that the *long-run* price elasticity of marketed surplus of food grains is positive. See Raj Krishna [58] and Behrman [16].

Marketed surplus also depends on cultivators' use of fertilizers in the sense that new inputs such as chemical fertilizers embody technical progress for traditional agriculture and shift the production functions so that the rise in output brought about by use of fertilizers raises farm sales of food (if farmers' marginal propensity to consume food is less than unity, more output will lead to more sales).

How much fertilizer farmers would use, of course, depends on the price of fertilizers they have to pay relative to the price of food at which they can sell their output, that is, on the ratio P_n/P_f. Thus,

$$N = N\left(\frac{P_n}{P_f}\right), \qquad N'\left(\frac{P_n}{P_f}\right) < 0. \tag{8}$$

When the fertilizer-crop price ratio rises, the farmers use less fertilizer. From (8), the prices P_f and P_n affect marketed surplus S in (7) in this indirect way as well.

The balance of trade between the industrial and the agricultural sector of the country is given by

$$P_f S = C_m^a + NP_n, \tag{9}$$

where C_m^a is the amount (and value) of textiles consumed by the agricultural sector. The left-hand side of (9) is the value of imports of food by the industrial sector from the agricultural sector and the right-hand side gives the value of its exports to the agricultural sector. It is to be noted that the government sells to the agricultural sector both its own output of fertilizers and all imported fertilizers at price P_n.

As for new investment, the choice is to invest in sector m (producing textiles or machines) and/or to invest in sector n (producing fertilizers). Once investment is made and capital is installed in a sector, however, it is assumed that it cannot be taken out and used in any other sector—the nonshiftability of capital assumption of Chapter 8. New investment is given by

$$\dot{K} = \dot{K}_m + \dot{K}_n = F_m + Z_m - C_m - C_m^a. \tag{10}$$

The extreme right-hand side of (10) gives the surplus of investible m available (through domestic production and imports) over consumption of m by both the industrial and the agricultural sectors.

$$\dot{K}_n = \lambda\dot{K} \qquad \text{and} \qquad \dot{K}_m = (1 - \lambda)\dot{K}, \tag{11}$$

where λ is the proportion (to be chosen) of new investment devoted to sector n.

It remains to specify the social objective function that the planner is supposed to maximize. We take it as

$$\max \int_0^T U(C_f, C_m)e^{-\rho t}\,dt + \alpha[K_m(T) + K_n(T)]e^{-\rho T}, \tag{12}$$

where U is a concave instantaneous utility function, ρ is a positive and constant rate of time discount, and α is a given constant (for simplification we are assuming that the planners give equal weight to the terminal capital stocks of the two types). The immediate objection to such a welfare function is that it ignores the welfare of the agricultural sector and only consumption in the industrial sector enters as arguments in the utility function. As the experienced reader must have surmised, this is our reluctant compromise with analytic tractability in this model of fairly complicated relationships. As a weak excuse, we might point out that in almost all of the dual-economy planning literature cited so far the welfare of the agricultural sector is ignored. For example, it is explicitly ignored in Marglin [62] and Dixit [29] and indirectly ignored by using objectives such as maximizing investment—as in Bose and Dixit [23]—or maximizing the steady-state rate of growth—as in Hornby [47]. The concentration on the industrial sector is intended mainly to bring out the implications of a policy of rapid industrialization in bold features.

9.2. OPTIMUM INVESTMENT AND TRADE POLICY

Taking all the constraints together we can now write our Hamiltonian H as given by

$$He^{\rho t} = U(C_f, C_m) - \gamma\left[Z_m + \bar{P}_f Z_f + \bar{P}_n\left\{N\left(\frac{P_n}{P_f}\right) - F_n(K_n, L_n)\right\}\right]e^{(\rho - r)t} + q\dot{K}, \tag{13}$$

where

$$C_f = S\left[P_f, N\left(\frac{P_n}{P_f}\right)\right] + Z_f$$

$$C_m = P_f[\overline{W}L - C_f] \qquad \text{and} \qquad L = L_m + L_n,$$

γ is a constant (as yet) undetermined multiplier,

$$\dot{K} = F_m(K_m, L_m) + Z_m + N\left(\frac{P_n}{P_f}\right)P_n - P_f \overline{W} L + P_f Z_f,$$

and

$$q = [\lambda q_n + (1 - \lambda) q_m],$$

where q_i is the imputed price of investment in industry producing the ith good ($i = m, n$). The Hamiltonian is to be maximized with respect to the control variables Z_f, Z_m, L_m, L_n, P_f, P_n, and λ. (We assume that both food and textiles are consumed and that both are produced in positive amounts in the industrial sector.) This immediately gives us the following first-order conditions

$$q - \gamma e^{(\rho - r)t} = 0 \tag{14}$$

$$(U_1 - U_2 P_f) + q(P_f - \bar{P}_f) = 0 \tag{15}$$

where

$$U_1 = \frac{\partial U}{\partial C_f} \quad \text{and} \quad U_2 = \frac{\partial U}{\partial C_m}$$

$$U_2 P_f \overline{W} + q\left[\frac{\partial F_m}{\partial L_m} - P_f \overline{W}\right] = 0 \tag{16}$$

$$U_2 P_f \overline{W} + q\left[\bar{P}_n \frac{\partial F_n}{\partial L_n} - P_f \overline{W}\right] = 0 \tag{17}$$

$$\frac{\partial S}{\partial P_f}(U_1 - U_2 P_f) - (U_2 - q)\frac{C_m}{P_f} - qS - qN'\left(\frac{P_n}{P_f}\right)\frac{P_n}{P_f^2}[P_n - \bar{P}_n] = 0 \tag{18}$$

$$\frac{\partial S}{\partial P_n}(U_1 - U_2 P_f) + qN + qN'\left(\frac{P_n}{P_f}\right)\frac{[P_n - \bar{P}_n]}{P_f} = 0 \tag{19}$$

$$\lambda \begin{cases} = 1 & \text{if } q_n > q_m \\ \varepsilon[0, 1] & \text{if } q_n = q_m \\ = 0 & \text{if } q_n < q_m. \end{cases} \tag{20}$$

The remaining necessary conditions are that $q_i(t)$ is continuous

($i = m, n$), satisfying

$$\dot{q}_n = \rho q_n - q\bar{P}_n \frac{\partial F_n}{\partial K_n} \tag{21}$$

$$\dot{q}_m = \rho q_m - q \frac{\partial F_m}{\partial K_m}. \tag{22}$$

The transversality conditions are that $q_m(T) = \alpha = q_m(T)$.

Let us now examine the implications of these optimality conditions.

Using (16), with positive marginal utility of consumption of textiles and positive shadow price of new investment q,

$$P_f \overline{W} > \frac{\partial F_m}{\partial L_m}. \tag{23}$$

This implies that the industrial wage rate is higher than the (value of) the marginal product of labor in industry m. In other words the optimum technique of production in industry m is more labor-intensive under our Ramsey-type social objective function than under the Galenson–Leibenstein [39] type of industrial surplus-maximizing policy (which equates industrial wage rate with marginal productivity of labor). This confirms the well-known Eckstein–Sen–Marglin result in the literature on choice of techniques. Equation (17) similarly implies that the industrial wage rate is higher than the marginal product of labor in industry n (valued at the world price of n).

From (17), (18), and (19),

$$[U_1 - U_2 P_f]\left[\frac{\partial S}{\partial P_f}\frac{P_f}{S} + \frac{\partial S}{\partial P_n}\frac{P_n}{S}\right]S = q\left[C_m^a + \frac{C_m}{P_f \overline{W}}\frac{\partial F_m}{\partial L_m}\right]. \tag{24}$$

If the shadow price of new investment q is positive, the right-hand side of (24) is positive.

Differentiating in (7), and using (8),

$$\left[\frac{\partial S}{\partial P_f}\frac{P_f}{S} + \frac{\partial S}{\partial P_n}\frac{P_n}{S}\right] = \frac{S_1 P_f}{S} > 0. \tag{25}$$

So, if $q > 0$, from (24),

$$U_1 - U_2 P_f > 0. \tag{26}$$

Using (26) in (15),[6]

$$\bar{P}_f - P_f > 0. \tag{27}$$

Equation (27) gives us an interesting result. It means that on the optimum path we should *subsidize* imports of food.[7] The essential reason for this result is as follows. The government as buyer of food has two sources to buy it from, the domestic agricultural sector and the foreign country. With respect to the former, the government's purchases affect the price, but this does not occur with respect to the foreign country. It follows from the theory of discriminating monopsony that the buyer tends to have a premium for buying from the more elastic source and in this case this represents the case for subsidizing imports of food from the foreign country.[8]

[6] One may note from the derivation of (27), that (27) holds even if $q < 0$.

[7] The point was first made by Hornby [47], p. 105. However, for two reasons his way of deriving this result might mislead a reader in regard to its essential rationale. (1) Hornby derives this result by maximizing the steady-state rate of growth; but as should be clear from our analysis above, the result has no connection with the steady state or even with any kind of dynamic model. It is purely an atemporal efficiency condition that follows from the theory of discriminating monopsony. (2) In his model Hornby discusses direct investment by the government in agriculture and he assumes that "the government makes no direct charge for the capital it invests in agriculture." This is not merely an empirically unsatisfactory assumption (it ignores water rates for irrigation, fertilizer prices, and so on, that the government charges in most countries and ignores the interesting problem concerning the determination of their optimum rates); theoretically, it might mislead the reader into thinking that this assumption might be responsible for the case for subsidizing food imports that he presents. This is possible for if one assumes that the government charges a positive rate (for simplification, assume that it is constant) for the capital it invests in agriculture, modifies Hornby's equation (16) in [47], p. 104, accordingly, and proceeds with maximization of the steady-state rate of growth, Hornby's result in regard to subsidization of food imports seems to disappear.

[8] What if instead of assuming that the foreign price of food is fixed we take the case in which more food imports bid up the foreign price, $\bar{P}_f$. In that case (15) will be changed to

$$(U_1 - U_2 P_f) + q\left[P_f - \bar{P}_f\left(1 + \frac{d\bar{P}_f}{dZ_f}\frac{Z_f}{\bar{P}_f}\right)\right] = 0.$$

This means that now we have no unambiguous case for subsidizing food imports. All we can say is that the optimum tariff on food imports, even when it is positive, is less than the optimum tariff in the standard literature (which is at a rate equal to the reciprocal of the price elasticity of food exports by the foreign country).

It is more difficult to obtain an unambiguous result in regard to the optimum trade policy with respect to imports of fertilizers. From (19), (24), and (25),

$$\operatorname{sign}(\bar{P}_n - P_n)N'\left(\frac{P_n}{P_f}\right)\frac{P_n}{P_f^2} =$$

$$\operatorname{sign}\left[\frac{NP_n}{C_m^a}\frac{S_1P_f}{S} + \frac{\partial S}{\partial P_n}\frac{P_n}{S}\left\{1 + \frac{C_m}{C_m^a P_f \overline{W}}\frac{\partial F_m}{\partial L_m}\right\}\right] \quad (28)$$

Let us define $(S_1P_f)/S = h_1$, which from (7) is the own price elasticity of marketed surplus of food (at a given level of fertilizer use). Let us also define $(S/P_n)(P_n/S) = -h_2$; from (7) and (8), h_2 is the (positively defined) elasticity of marketed surplus of food with respect to changes in fertilizer price. Actually h_2 is the product of three elasticities, the elasticity of marketed surplus of food with respect to food output (which, with income elasticity of demand for food less than unity, is larger than one), the elasticity of food crop output with respect to use of fertilizers (which at present low levels of chemical fertilizer use in most countries with traditional agriculture is very high, as indicated by available data[9] of output response to fertilizer trials conducted on farms), and the (positively defined) elasticity of fertilizer use with respect to its price. It seems that in developing economies h_2 is likely to be very high, particularly at low levels of chemical fertilizer use. If h_2 is larger than or equal to h_1,[10] and if $NP_n/C_m^a < 1$ [which means, from (9), that in the industrial sectors' exports to the agricultural sector, sales of consumer goods (textiles) exceed those of agricultural inputs (fertilizers)—which is also in general likely to be true], then the right-hand side of (28) is negative, so that $\bar{P}_n - P_n > 0$. Under these circumstances the government should also *subsidize* imports of fertilizers. It should be kept in mind that this holds only under a set of very special assumptions, and that these assumptions (such as $h_2 \geq h_1$ and $NP_n/C_m^a < 1$) are more likely to be valid at low levels of fertilizer use. As the agrarian economy becomes more prosperous (so that h_1 becomes

[9] For such data for India, see Panse [73]; for data for China, see Jung-Chao Liu [61].

[10] The value of h_1 is likely to be low in poor agrarian economies, because when the price of a food crop P_f goes up, farmers' income goes up and even if their income elasticity of demand for food grains is less than unity, it is still quite high (it is about 0.6 in rural India according to National Sample Survey data) and the farmers tend to retain a large proportion of their increased output.

large), and as a substantial quantity of chemical fertilizers is absorbed in crop production (so that h_2 is not very high and NP_n/C^a_m is larger than before), one can conceivably have a case for taxing imports of fertilizers.

Essentially, the question is whether the government should subsidize or tax sales of the domestically produced intermediate good (fertilizer) to the agricultural sector. On the one hand, it should tax it (thus improving the industrial sector's terms of trade with the agricultural sector), but on the other, cheaper fertilizer means improved productivity in agriculture (and thus better terms of trade for industry). In the initial stages of development, that is, at a low level of fertilizer use, the latter productivity effect dominates and presents a case for subsidy. This suggests, as Max Corden pointed out to me, that the optimum tariff in the standard literature may be negative if the country exports a productivity-raising intermediate product used in producing exportables in the foreign country.

We have so far tried to discover the implications of our optimality conditions for choice of production techniques and for trade policy. Let us now briefly turn to optimal investment policy in this model.

The first thing to note is that although we started with smooth neoclassical production functions for the industrial sector, all along the optimum path only one technique (capital-labor ratio) will be used in each industry. Let us explain this.

Since production functions are subject to constant returns to scale in each industry, the marginal product of each factor is a function only of the capital-labor ratio used in an industry. From (16) and (17),

$$\bar{P}_n = \frac{\dfrac{\partial F_m}{\partial L_m}}{\dfrac{\partial F_n}{\partial L_n}}. \tag{29}$$

Equation (29) gives K_m/L_m, the capital-labor ratio in industry m, as a unique function of K_n/L_n, the capital-labor ratio in industry n. Now if $q_n = q_m = q$, then from (21) and (22)

$$\bar{P}_n = \frac{\dfrac{\partial F_m}{\partial K_m}}{\dfrac{\partial F_n}{\partial K_n}}. \tag{30}$$

Equations (29) and (30) imply that K_m/L_m and K_n/L_n are constant, so that on the optimal path only one technique will be used in each industry. If $q = q_m > q_n$, then from (14) and (22),

$$\frac{\partial F_m}{\partial K_m} = r, \tag{31}$$

where r is the given rate of interest at which the country can borrow to cover its deficit in balance of trade. From (29) and (30), again K_m/L_m and K_n/L_n are fixed. If $q = q_n > q_m$, then from (14) and (21),

$$\bar{P}_n \frac{\partial F_n}{\partial K_n} = r. \tag{32}$$

Equations (29) and (32) again imply that K_m/L_m and K_n/L_n are fixed.

This result concerning the constancy of technique in industrial production follows essentially from the constant world relative price of the industrial goods[11] and the world interest rate.

Since they are constant, let us define $\bar{P}_n(\partial F_n/\partial K_n) = a$ and $\partial F_m/\partial K_m = b$. We shall now see that the optimum investment policy depends on the relative values of a and b. With the help of (14) we can now integrate (21) and (22) and obtain

$$q_n(t) = e^{\rho t}\left[q_n(0) - \frac{a\gamma}{r}(1 - e^{-rt})\right] \tag{33}$$

$$q_m(t) = e^{\rho t}\left[q_m(0) - \frac{b\gamma}{r}(1 - e^{-rt})\right]. \tag{34}$$

From the transversality conditions $q_m(T) = \alpha = q_n(T)$, we can obtain the values of $q_n(0)$ and $q_m(0)$ and hence (33) and (34) may be rewritten as

$$q_n(t) = e^{\rho t}\left[\alpha e^{-\rho T} + \frac{a\gamma}{r}(e^{-rt} - e^{-rT})\right] \tag{35}$$

$$q_m(t) = e^{\rho t}\left[\alpha e^{-\rho T} + \frac{b\gamma}{r}(e^{-rt} - e^{-rT})\right]. \tag{36}$$

[11] The same result holds even when the world price of n changes with changes in the home country's imports of n but if the price elasticity of the rest of the world's export of n is constant.

It is immediately obvious from (35) and (36) that for any $t < T$:

(i) If $a > b$, that is, the constant marginal product of capital (valued at world prices) is larger for the industry producing fertilizers, then $q_n(t) > q_m(t)$, so that from (20), $\lambda = 1$, that is, all new investment should be devoted to the fertilizer industry.

(ii) If $a = b$, then $q_n(t) = q_m(t) = q(t)$, so that from (20), $1 > \lambda > 0$, that is, new investment should go to both the industries.

(iii) If $a < b$, $q_n(t) < q_m(t)$, so that $\lambda = 0$, that is, all new investment should go to the industry producing textiles and machines.

Before concluding we might extend the model in two ways. First, we can modify the instantaneous utility function in (12) by introducing the magnitude of industrial employment L as a separate argument in the utility function so that

$$U = U(C_f, C_m, L), \qquad \text{with} \quad U_3 = \frac{\partial U}{\partial L} > 0. \tag{37}$$

Equation (37) implies that in the social objective function a positive weight is attached to the size of the industrial labor force (maybe because of unemployment in the countryside or in nonindustrial service sectors). The reader can confirm that this will not alter any of the results mentioned in this section; in fact, all of them will be reinforced if we assume $U_3 > 0$.

One might also consider a strong argument for including L as a determinant of S in (7). This means that an addition to the industrial labor force achieved by reducing the size of the agricultural population may affect the surplus of food marketed. Thus, we may have

$$S = S(P_f, N, L). \tag{38}$$

It is, however, difficult to be unambiguous about the sign of $S_3 = \partial S/\partial L$. If marginal productivity of labor in the agricultural sector is low, then transfer of labor from the agricultural to the industrial sector is likely to raise the marketed surplus of food, because with farmers' income elasticity of demand less than unity an increase in their per capita income is likely to raise their sales, so that $S_3 > 0$. As fertilizers and other new current inputs (such as improved seeds) bring technical progress of a kind that is land-saving and labor-using, however, it may not be appropriate to assume that labor's marginal productivity in agriculture is or will remain low.

How are our results affected? The results concerning optimal investment policy are unaltered. If S_3, whether positive or negative, is small in absolute value the results related to subsidization of imports of food and fertilizers and techniques of production being more labor-intensive than under a surplus maximization still hold. Our results concerning subsidization of imports of food will hold even if S_3 has a large negative value.

REFERENCES

[1] Amano, A., "Determinants of Comparative Costs," *Oxford Economic Papers*, Vol. N.S. 16 (November 1964).

[2] Arrow, K. J., "The Economic Implications of Learning by Doing," *Review of Economic Studies*, Vol. 29 (June 1962).

[3] Arrow, K. J. "Applications of Control Theory to Economic Growth," in *Mathematics of Decision Sciences*, Part II, American Mathematical Society, 1969.

[4] Arrow, K. J., Chenery, H. B., Minhas, B. S., and Solow, R. M., "Capital–Labor Substitution and Economic Efficiency," *Review of Economics and Statistics*, Vol. 43 (August 1961).

[5] Baldwin, R., "Equilibrium in International Trade: A Diagrammatic Analysis," *Quarterly Journal of Economics*, Vol. 62 (November 1948).

[6] Ball, D. S., "Factor Intensity Reversals in International Comparison of Factor Costs and Factor Use," *Journal of Political Economy*, Vol. 74 (February 1966).

[7] Bardhan, P. K., "External Economics, Economic Development and the Theory of Protection," *Oxford Economic Papers*, Vol. N.S. 16 (March 1964).

[8] Bardhan, P. K., "International Differences in Production Functions, Trade and Factor Prices," *Economic Journal*, Vol. 75 (March 1965).

[9] Bardhan, P. K., "On Factor Accumulation and the Pattern of International Specialization," *Review of Economic Studies*, Vol. 33 (January 1966).

[10] Bardhan, P. K., "Optimum Accumulation and International Trade," *Review of Economic Studies*, Vol. 32 (July 1965).

[11] Bardhan, P. K., "Equilibrium Growth in the International Economy," *Quarterly Journal of Economics*, Vol. 79 (August 1965).
[12] Bardhan, P. K., "On Factor-Biased Technical Progress and International Trade," *Journal of Political Economy*, Vol. 73 (August 1965).
[13] Bardhan, P. K., "International Trade Theory in a Vintage Capital Model," *Econometrica*, Vol. 34 (October 1966).
[14] Bardhan, P. K., "Equilibrium Growth with Economic Obsolescence of Machines," *Quarterly Journal of Economics*, Vol. 89 (May 1969).
[15] Bardhan, P. K., "Optimum Foreign Borrowing," in K. Shell (ed.) [88].
[16] Behrman, J. R., "Price Elasticity of the Marketed Surplus of a Subsistence Crop," *Journal of Farm Economics*, Vol. 48 (November 1966).
[17] Bensusan-Butt, D. M., "A Model of Trade and Accumulation," *American Economic Review*, Vol. 44 (September 1954).
[18] Bhagwati, J., "Immiserizing Growth: A Geometrical Note," *Review of Economic* Studies, Vol. 25 (June 1958).
[19] Bhagwati, J., "The Pure Theory of International Trade: A Survey," *Economic Journal*, Vol. 74 (March 1964).
[20] Bhagwati, J., and Ramaswami, V. K., "Domestic Distortions, Tariffs, and the Theory of Optimum Subsidy," *Journal of Political Economy*, Vol. 71 (February 1963).
[21] Bose, S., "Optimal Growth and Investment Allocation," *Review of Economic Studies*, Vol. 35 (October 1968).
[22] Bose, S., "Optimal Growth in a Non-Shiftable Capital Model," *Econometrica*, Vol. 38 (January 1970).
[23] Bose, S., and Dixit, A., "Development Planning: A Theoretical Analysis," Holden-Day, forthcoming.
[24] Cass, D., "Optimal Growth in an Aggregative Model of Capital Accumulation," *Review of Economic Studies*, Vol. 32 (July 1965).
[25] Caves, R. E., *Trade and Economic Structure*, Harvard University Press, 1960.
[26] Chipman, J. S., "Survey of the Theory of International Trade," Part III, *Econometrica*, Vol. 34 (January 1966).
[27] Clague, C., "An International Comparison of Industrial Efficiency: Peru and the United States," *Review of Economics and Statistics*, Vol. 49 (November 1967).
[28] Diaz-Alejandro, C., "Industrialization and Labour Productivity Differentials," *Review of Economics and Statistics*, Vol. 47 (May 1965).
[29] Dixit, A. K., "Optimal Development in the Labour-Surplus Economy," *Review of Economic Studies*, Vol. 35 (January 1968).
[30] Dobb, M., *An Essay on Economic Growth and Planning*, Routledge & Kegan Paul, 1960.
[31] Domer, E. D., "A Soviet Model of Growth," in *Essays in the Theory of Economic Growth*, Oxford University Press, 1967.
[32] Eckstein, O., "Investment for Economic Development and the Theory of Intertemporal Welfare Economics," *Quarterly Journal of Economics*, Vol. 71 (February 1957).
[33] Edgeworth, F. Y., "The Theory of International Values, I," *Economic Journal*, Vol. 4 (March 1894) (reprinted in [34]).

[34] Edgeworth, F. Y., *Papers Relating to Political Economy*, Vol. II, Macmillan, 1925.

[35] Fel'dman, G. A., "On the Theory of Growth Rates of National Income," translated in N. Spulber (ed.), *Foundations of Soviet Strategy for Economic Growth*, Indiana University Press, 1964.

[36] Findlay, R., "Capital Theory and Development Planning," *Review of Economic Studies*, Vol. 29 (February 1962).

[37] Findlay, R., and Grubert, H., "Factor Intensity, Technological Progress and the Terms of Trade," *Oxford Economic Papers*, Vol. N.S. 11 (February 1959).

[38] Gale, D., and Nikaidô, H., "The Jacobian Matrix and Global Univalence of Mappings," *Mathematische Annalen*, Vol. 159 (1965).

[39] Galenson, W., and Leibenstein, H., "Investment Criteria, Productivity and Economic Development," *Quarterly Journal of Economics*, Vol. 69 (August 1955).

[40] Graaff, J. de V., *Theoretical Welfare Economics*, Cambridge University Press, 1957.

[41] Guha, A., "Factor and Commodity Prices in an Expanding Economy," *Quarterly Journal of Economics*, Vol. 77 (February 1963).

[42] Haberler, G., *A Survey of International Trade Theory*, Special Papers in International Economics, Princeton University Press (Rev. Ed.), 1961.

[43] Hahn, F. H., and Matthews, R. C. O., "The Theory of Economic Growth; A Survey," *Economic Journal*, Vol. 74 (December 1964).

[44] Hamada, K., "Economic Growth and Long-Term International Capital Movements," *Yale Economic Essays*, Vol. 6 (Spring 1966).

[45] Harrod, R. F., "Factor-Price Relations Under Free Trade," *Economic Journal*, Vol. 68 (June 1958).

[46] Hirsch, W. Z., "Firm Progress Ratios," *Econometrica*, Vol. 24 (April 1956).

[47] Hornby, J. N., "Investment and Trade Policy in the Dual Economy," *Economic Journal*, Vol. 78 (March 1968).

[48] Johansen, L., "Some Theoretical Properties of a Two-Sector Model of Optimal Growth," *Review of Economic Studies*, Vol. 34 (January 1967).

[49] Johnson, H. G., *International Trade and Economic Growth*, Allen & Unwin, 1958.

[50] Johnson, H. G., "International Trade, Income Distribution and the Offer Curve," *Manchester School of Economics and Social Studies*, Vol. 27 (September 1959).

[51] Johnson, H. G., *Money, Trade and Economic Growth: Survey Lectures in Economic Theory* (2nd Ed.), Unwin University Books, 1964.

[52] Johnson, H. G., *Comparative Cost and Commercial Policy Theory for a Developing World Economy*, Wicksell Lectures, Almqvist & Wicksell, 1968.

[53] Jorgenson, D. W., "The Development of a Dual Economy," *Economic Journal*, Vol. 71 (June 1961).

[54] Kemp, M. C., *The Pure Theory of International Trade*, Prentice-Hall, 1964.

[55] Kenen, P. B., "Nature, Capital and Trade," *Journal of Political Economy*, Vol. 73 (October 1965).

[56] Khang, C., "A Neoclassical Growth Model of a Resource-Poor Open Economy," *International Economic Review*, Vol. 9 (October 1968).

[57] Kindleberger, C. P., *Foreign Trade and the National Economy*, Yale University Press, 1962.

[58] Krishna, R., "A Note on the Elasticity of the Marketable Surplus of a Subsistence Crop," *Indian Journal of Agricultural Economics*, Vol. 17, (July–September 1962).

[59] Lancaster, K., *Mathematical Economics*, Macmillan, 1968.

[60] Leontief, W., "An International Comparison of Factor Costs and Factor Use," *American Economic Review*, Vol. 54 (June 1964).

[61] Liu, J. C., "Fertilizer Application in Communist China," *China Quarterly*, No. 24 (October–December 1965).

[62] Marglin, S. A., "The Rate of Interest and the Value of Capital with Unlimited Supplies of Labor," in K. Shell (ed.) [88].

[63] Marshall, A., *The Pure Theory of Foreign Trade*, 1879, reprinted with *The Pure Theory of Domestic Values*, London School of Economics and Political Science, 1930.

[64] Meade, J. E., *Trade and Welfare*, Oxford University Press, 1955.

[65] Minabe, N., "The Stolper–Samuelson Theorem, the Rybczynski Effect, and the Heckscher–Ohlin Theory of Trade Pattern and Factor Price Equalization," *Canadian Journal of Economics and Political Science*, Vol 33 (August 1967).

[66] Minhas, B. S., *International Comparisons of Factor Costs and Factor Use*, North Holland, 1963.

[67] Mishan, E. J., "International Factor Price Determination with Neutral Technical Progress," *Economica*, Vol. N.S. 33 (August 1966).

[68] Mohalanobis, P. C., "Some Observations on the Process of Growth of National Income," *Sankhya* (Indian Journal of Statistics), Vol. 15 (September 1953).

[69] Mohalanobis, P. C., "Science and National Planning," *Sankhya* (Indian Journal of Statistics), Vol. 20 (September 1958).

[70] Nakamura, J. I., *Agricultural Production and the Economic Development of Japan, 1873–1922*, Princeton University Press, 1966.

[71] Nelson, R. R., and Phelps, E. S., "Investment in Humans, Technological Diffusion and Eeconomic Growth," *American Economic Review*, Vol. 56 (May 1966).

[72) Oniki, H., and Uzawa, H., "Patterns of Trade and Investment in a Dynamic Model of International Trade," *Review of Economic Studies*, Vol. 32 (January 1965).

[73] Panse, V. G., "Fertilizer Recommendations," in *Proceedings of the National Seminar on Fertilizers*, Fertilizer Association of India, 1965.

[74] Pontryagin, L. S., et al., *The Mathematical Theory of Optimal Processes*, John Wiley, 1962.

[75] Preobrazhensky, E., *The New Economics* (translated by B. Pearce), Clarendon Press, 1965.

[76] Raj, K. N., "The Role of the Machine-Tools Sector in Economic Growth,"

in C. H. Feinstein (ed.), *Socialism, Capitalism and Economic Growth*, Essays Presented to Maurice Dobb, Cambridge University Press, 1967.

[77] Raj, K. N., and Sen, A. K., "Alternative Patterns of Growth under Conditions of Stagnant Export Earnings," *Oxford Economic Papers*, Vol. N.S. 13 (February 1961).

[78] Ramsey, F. P., "A Mathematical Theory of Savings," *Economic Journal*, Vol. 38 (December 1928).

[79] Ranis, G., and Fei, J. C. H., "A Theory of Economic Development," *American Economic Review*, Vol. 51 (June 1961).

[80] Rybczynski, T., "Factor Endowment and Relative Commodity Prices," *Economica*, Vol. 22 (November 1955).

[81] Ryder, H. E., "Optimal Accumulation and Trade in an Open Economy of Moderate Size," in K. Shell (ed.) [88].

[82] Salter, W. E. G., *Productivity and Technical Change*, Cambridge University Press, 1960.

[83] Samuelson, P. A., "International Factor Price Equalization Once Again," *Economic Journal*, Vol. 59 (June 1949) (reprinted in [85]).

[84] Samuelson, P. A., "Prices of Factors and Goods in General Equilibrium," *Review of Economic Studies*, Vol. 21 (1953–54) (reprinted with a postscript in [85]).

[85] Samuelson, P. A., *The Collected Scientific Papers of Paul A. Samuelson, Vol. I*, M.I.T. Press, 1966.

[86] Sen, A. K., *Choice of Techniques*, Basil Blackwell, 1960.

[87] Sen, A. K., "On the Usefulness of Used Machines," *Review of Economics and Statistics*, Vol. 44 (August 1962).

[88] Shell, K. (ed.), *Essays on the Theory of Optimal Economic Growth*, M.I.T. Press, 1967.

[89] Solow, R. M., "Substitution and Fixed Proportions in the Theory of Capital," *Review of Economic Studies*, Vol. 29 (July 1962).

[90] Solow, R. M., Tobin, J., von Weizsäcker, C., and Yaari, M., "Neoclassical Growth with Fixed Factor Proportions," *Review of Economic Studies*, Vol. 33 (April 1966).

[91] Tobin, J., "Liquidity Preference as a Behavior towards Risk," *Review of Economic Studies*, Vol. 25 (February 1958).

[92] Tobin, J., "Money and Economic Growth," *Econometrica*, Vol. 33 (October 1965).

[93] Uzawa, H., "Optimal Growth in a Two-Sector Model of Capital Accumulation," *Review of Economic Studies*, Vol. 31 (January 1964).

[94] Wright, T. P., "Factors Affecting the Cost of Airframes," *Journal of the Aeronautical Sciences*, Vol. 3 (February 1936).

INDEX